STEP BY STEP
GOALTENDING

Interested readers may consult our ever-evolving catalogue
on the World-Wide Web:

http:www.rdppub.com

Jacques Plante

STEP BY STEP GOALTENDING

STUDIO 9 BOOKS

Ordering information:

United States:
Studio 9 Books, 162 Margaret Street, Plattsburgh, NY 12901
☎ 518-298-8595
Also available from Koen, Baker & Taylor and Ingram

Canada:
Starbooks Distribution
100 Armstrong Ave., Georgetown, Ontario L7G 5S4
Tel 905-877-4411, Fax 877-4410,
☎ (905) 877-2828 📠 (905) 877-4410 SAN: 118-8801
E-mail: sales@starbooks.ca

or from the publisher (special & group orders):
Studio 9 Books
Montreal, QC H3H 1A7, Canada
☎ 514-934-5433 📠 514-937-8765
e-mail: mail2@rdppub.com

UK, Ireland, Europe (France excepted):
Worlwide Book Distribution,
Unit 9, Oakwood Industrial Park,
Gatwick Road, Crawley, West Sussex RH10 9AZ
☎ 44-1293-456300 📠44-1293-536644

France:
Éditions Casteilla,
10 rue Léon Foucault, 78184 St-Quentin-en Yvelines Cedex
☎ 01-3014-1930 📠 01-3460-3132

We wish to thank the Sodec (Québec) and the Department of Canadian Heritage
(BPIDP) for their generous support of our publishing program.

CONTENTS

Publisher's note

Jacques Plante was one of the greatest goaltenders ever to play the game of hockey. A star in the National Hockey League for many years with the Montreal Canadiens, then with the Toronto Maple Leafs, Jacques Plante was also aware of the dangers inherent in playing goal, and pioneered the goalie's mask, now universally used in the sport. Jacques Plante also was particularly attentive to the needs of young players, and spent a considerable amount of his time mentoring at hockey camps in several countries. If one of his legacies is the mask, another is unquestionably the higher quality of play of netminders, thanks to ideas he developed and taught, and in a modest way, thanks to this book, which codified techniques and exercises that led the way up.

Hockey lost a great friend, and a great champion, when Jacques Plante died, much too young, at age 57 in 1986. This new edition returns to the current generation of hockey players and enthusiasts a book which had been unavailable for many years, and the publishers hope it will help the name of Jacques Plante live on into the new millenium.

PREFACE

For years I have talked about the necessity for each coach to establish a system between his goalie and the defense, so that together they can more easily contain the offense.

You have no idea of all the things a goalie needs to remember—and do—to play well; but when he knows what his defense will do against every offensive formation, his work becomes much easier because he then moves freely, without fear of being caught out of position.

The more prominent a person is in any field, the more he is subject to criticism. When a hockey team loses, which player is most often criticized? You guessed it: the goalie. (Is he not worth between 50 and 60 per cent of his team?) And most of the time, the spectators don't have the slightest idea of where the mistake was made on the goal ... because for every goal, there is a mistake made.

From now on, if you have a tendency to point the finger at the goalie, try to replay each goal (it should be easy on television) and you will notice that the goalie is seldom guilty. Watch what goes on in front of the net and you'll get a better idea of why the goal went in.

Put yourself in the goalie's spot, facing shots traveling at over a hundred miles an hour, with players pushing you, interfering with you, or skating in all directions in front of the net, trying to screen you or to deflect the puck. How would you, first, look for the puck; second, follow it; third, position yourself to stop it; and fourth, catch it or deflect it away from the front of the net?

Remember that the goalie has only a split second to decide what to do and how to do it. If he is wrong and misses, there is no second chance.

Pressure is the name of the game. The stronger the team he plays against, the more pressure a goalie feels—the kind of tension that produces ulcers and has forced some great goalies to quit the game—goalies like Wilf Cude, Frank McCool, Bill Durnan, Gerry McNeil.

Roger Crozier said, "There is no way people will understand our particular kind of pressure. Anyone who isn't a goaltender probably won't experience once what we experience hundreds of times; even the other players don't know what the goalie goes through in a game."

Wilf Cude once told me when I visited him in Rouen, Quebec, that one day he was so tense, thinking of the game he had to play that night, that he threw his steak at his wife. After it hit the wall, he couldn't believe what he had done, and not long after that, he decided he had had enough of this life and retired. I've often wondered since then how he would react to today's slap shots and curved sticks.

And how about "Mister Goalie," Glenn Hall? I can still see him on game night, deathly ill, burping, swallowing hard, and holding a towel in front of his mouth, just in case he couldn't make it in time to the bathroom. His nerves were so bad that he often left in the middle of a game to throw up. To this day, I can't understand how he lasted so long and played so well under these conditions.

Tony Esposito calls it "plain torture." Like all goalies, he is afraid to play badly. He doesn't fear getting hurt, but he thinks about it. So do 1. Since injuries occur mostly during practices, we can never relax and take it easy. "The pressure," Tony says, "is always there, one way or another."

A goalie depends so much on his teammates' playing that at times it gets on his nerves and he loses his temper. Goalies are a breed apart because of the work they do and because no one else can understand what they go through before and during a game. After the game, they often have to explain what happened on many goals. Most of the time they accept the blame, because it is their job to stop the puck, but when they point out another player's error, they are called poor losers, trying to find excuses for their mistake.

To succeed, goalies have to have desire, pride in their work, a lot of ability—more than any other player—good judgment, steel nerves, and a high degree of resistance to endure all the injuries they suffer during the course of a season.

After reading this book, you'll never be able to watch another hockey game without asking yourself:

"How can they do it?"

FOREWORD

If you look at me today, you'll notice a lot of grey hair, which is often the sign of wisdom. Maybe that's true in my case. Certainly, it took me long enough to get where I am, and I don't think I could have done better than I did.

For more than thirty years I acquired experience, but I kept secret most of what I learned, so opposing players and goalies couldn't benefit from my findings. I must have mellowed, because now I'm ready to let you in on all my secrets.

In this book you will learn how and why you must play a certain way and be able to correct yourself as you go along.

This book is a guide that you should read and re-read often, not go through just once and leave on a shelf to gather dust. Keep it handy and return to it at least once a month during the season. Read a few pages at a time and compare with your way of playing. It's easy to forget certain moves and not know what we're doing wrong.

Remember that goaltending is an art. To master it, you have to continuously adjust your style to conserve energy and remain strong until the end of each game, and consequently play better. You have to read, observe, listen, question, and practice every time the occasion is given you.

All my life I learned through my mistakes because I had no one who could help me. You don't have that problem. But you'll discover that goalies aren't made in a day. You have to grow up, mature, and suffer a multitude of setbacks and defeats before you're a great goalie. And even then, the work doesn't stop.

At age 44, I'm still learning. The game has changed a lot over the years, and I've had to adjust my style, as you must, to keep up with the new rules, new offensive formations, new pieces of equipment. I've seen the introduction of the red line at center ice in 1943; the slap shots in the late 'forties; the curved sticks in the 'sixties. What will come up next? Nobody knows. But I can assure you that it will not favor the goalies. So be prepared to adjust your style once more when it happens.

Goaltenders are a small group of young and not-so-young artists who, besides doing their own work, have to correct everybody else's mistakes. The hardest thing is to get started on the right foot. All too often they are unable to succeed because no one ever taught them how. Too many coaches don't have any idea of what goaltending is all about and then wonder why their goalies don't improve as fast as they think they should.

Originally, goaltending was played "by ear" by what I call the finest craftsmen of hockey. They were not admired then as much as today, because few people realized what their work really involved.

The expansion brought sharply into focus that the NHL, in its rapid growth, had paid too little attention to the quality of its minor league clubs, many of whom were interested only in winning championships rather than teaching the game to youngsters.

The expansion brought sharply into focus the fact that the NHL, in its rapid growth, had paid too little attention to the quality of its minor league clubs, many of whom were interested only in winning championships rather than teaching the game to youngsters.

Totally new formations are being executed in the NHL, and offensive plays have become very sophisticated. The offensive formations have improved so fast that the defensive end of the game has not kept up.

The true greatness of a defensive play is in the simplicity of its execution. Yet there are standard defensive requirements that are

not seen enough nowadays. Most team effort is focused on pro-
ducing a devastating attack. It is difficult in a few words and
drawings to convey the importance of playing positional hockey.
But if I can give you even one helpful tip this book was worth
writing.

1 SO YOU WANT TO BE A GOALIE

A dedicated goaltender prides himself not only on the number of saves he makes, but also on the quality of the saves. No other athlete has to remember so many things in such a short space of time. A mistake usually costs you a goal.

To play well, you must have, first, the talent and, second, the desire to play. How good you will be depends on the degree of your talent and the time you are willing to put into the game. Your size has little to do with it, although a tall goaltender like Ken Dryden covers more room and usually has more success, especially nowadays, with ever-increasing use of slap shots. (When I started, only one or two players per team had a good shot. Today, more than half the players in the NHL can score from fifty feet out if the goalie isn't very careful.)

Oh, you'll goof once in a while—who doesn't—but try not to make a habit of it. You must firmly believe that you can stop every shot or you'll never be an A-1 goalie. If you become convinced that some shots from a certain distance or speed are impossible to stop, you will use this as an excuse instead of trying to find out why a goal was scored.

You'll meet two kinds of coaches during your career: The ones who shout and criticize, and the teachers. The ones who run practices to help you, not just to make the other players skate and try to score goals. But no matter which type they are, they will prefer to repeat their instructions ten times rather than hear you say, "I understand," when you don't. If the verbal explanations don't register, ask your coach to use the blackboard. If that's still not enough, ask him to show you on the ice. Then, after you understand, go to work. Don't worry too much if you repeat that mistake. Time and practice make perfect, and the more you practice, the faster you'll overcome your weaknesses.

Communications between you and your coach are of utmost importance. If you feel your coach criticizes you too much, let him know how much pressure he is putting on you and how it affects your game. If he cares about the team, he'll change.

Unfortunately, the days are gone when hockey was played without the constant emphasis on winning. The sport is so organized now that the pressure is always on. Playing for coaches who want only to win championships is no fun, and it's really tough on the young ones. That's why many of them quit at fourteen or fifteen. They have been regimented since the age of five and want out.

Those who can stick with it despite the pressure are the dedicated ones. Are you one of them? Try to communicate with your teachers, parents and coaches. You may find that even in our high-velocity world, people can still take the time to lend a helping hand to those who know how to ask—especially your coaches. Don't they spend most of their spare time coaching you?

And speaking of pressure, no other player feels the same degree of tension that a goalie does. The hardest shots take a half a second to zip from the blue line to the net; you blink your eyes and it's a goal. You might think it will be a high shot, but if it isn't, you're beat before you realize what happened. Check your watch—see how fast a half a second is.

There will be even more pressure when you play against the strong teams. You may feel sick to your stomach. You may start shaking as though you're freezing. Most of the time, the feeling will stop once the game begins. But if it doesn't and it happens too often, you'll have to quit the game as a number of goalies have when the pressure has led to ulcers.

Sometimes you'll sit in the dressing room wondering, "What am

I doing here?" and ask yourself why you became a goalie. The other players can laugh and joke while you suffer, worrying about the outcome of the game. They can't think the way you do, so they don't feel the same pressure. When they make a mistake, they may apologize to you, but when they say, "I'm sorry," it's too late; a goal has already been scored. You can't say a thing when the referee picks up the puck while all eyes in the rink focus on you, as if to say, "It's his fault. Why didn't he make the save"? The fans may boo you when too many goals go in. Be prepared for it. You won't like it, but a goalie has to learn to live with it. It goes with the job.

As you mature, the press, radio, and T.V. will cover your games. You won't always agree with their reports, but never let your temper get the best of you. Remind yourself that what a sportswriter says is strictly his own opinion, and not necessarily the fans'. Never criticize the press; cooperate with them. It's as much a part of your work as it is theirs to ask questions.

If after all this you should make it to the NHL, you'll find it a unique experience. Imagine playing against more than two hundred of the most highly trained, knowledgeable experts in hockey, which in itself is a memorable, enriching—if sobering—experience. Players with bullet shots are in abundance, and you'll sometimes feel like you're standing in the middle of swinging doors.

Reaching the NHL is possible only for those with exceptional talent who can produce to the utmost of their ability. You have to make it on your own, and build yourself a reputation for being tops. You don't want people pointing at you and yelling, "Hey, what are you doing in this league?"

You'll discover, as Tony Esposito said so well, "Playing goal is pressure." You get it from your coach, the players, your parents, the fans, the members of the media and from the game itself; the danger of injuries, the desire to win, the fear of playing badly and losing. But even with all this I've loved every minute of it and wouldn't have wanted my life to be any other way. I still think that playing goal is the best position in hockey. The rewarding moments made up for all the aggravation and the bad days.

Now that you know what to expect, and if you still want to play goal, do it. But first, set yourself some goals to reach and take them one at the time. That's the only way you'll succeed. Never hesitate to ask for advice; work to improve yourself, and try to be more relaxed when you play. Winning is only half the fun. Just playing is the other.

The last of the unmasked goaltenders — Lorne "Gump" Worsley

2 HOW TO EXERCISE AT HOME

As a goaltender, you should exercise even more than other players. Very often, you have only a split second to make a save, and your muscles must respond. They are pulled in all directions and, if not in good working condition, they stretch too much and tear, causing an injury. You really punish your body each time you play, so keep it strong by regular exercise.

If your body is in shape, your mind will also be more alert. Knowledge and experience are wasted if you are so tired that you lose your concentration.

The following exercises will condition your muscles if repeated daily a month before training camp. It is not easy to train alone, but remember: "You only harvest what you sow." I recommend you continue to exercise ten minutes daily all season long. If you do, you'll find a big difference in your game.

NECK

1. Clasp hands over your forehead and push your head forward as hard as you can, counting five. Repeat three times.

2. Clasp hands against the back of your head and push your head backward as hard as you can, counting five. Repeat three times.

3. Rotate your head from left to right and right to left five times. Repeat three times.

BACK

1. Lie on your stomach with your hands on the floor. Push up to make an arch with your back, keeping your head up. Then lift the seat as high as possible, push back, and put your head down. Do not bend your knees. Repeat eight times.

Back Exercise 1, first part

**Back Exercise 1,
second part**

2. Lie on your stomach and hold your hands behind your back. Lift your head and legs at the same time, forming an arch with your back. Repeat eight times.

SHOULDERS

1. Standing up, lock hands at shoulder height. Pull as hard as you can, counting three. Repeat five times.

2. In the same stance, push one fist against the other hand. Push as hard as you can, counting three. Repeat five times.

STOMACH

1. Lie on your back with your hands on your thighs. Slide them to your knees as often as you can for fifteen seconds. Repeat three times.

2. Lie on your back with your feet under a bed and your hands holding the back of your head. Sit up as often as you can for fifteen seconds. Repeat three times.

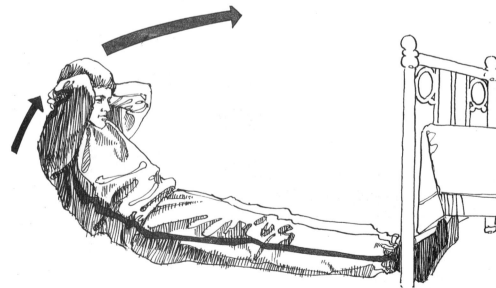

3. Lie on your back with your legs on a chair and your hands behind your head. Touch your right knee with your left elbow, then the left knee with the right elbow, as often as you can for fifteen seconds. Repeat three times.

4. Lie on your back with your hands behind your head. Lift your legs six inches from the floor, spread them slowly as far as you can, bring them back together, and lower them to the floor. Repeat five times.

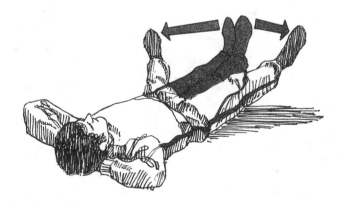

LEGS

Your legs are your bread and butter, so be very careful when you exercise them. Never do exercises such as knee bends or squats that pull the bones out of their sockets.

Thighs

Working with weights is very good if you keep your legs straight. I usually exercise at night with a sixteen-pound lead foot while watching T.V. I lift the weight each time there is a commercial and change legs every hour.

When I exercise during the day, I read a book and lift the weight three times with each page I read; this helps break the monotony of the exercises.

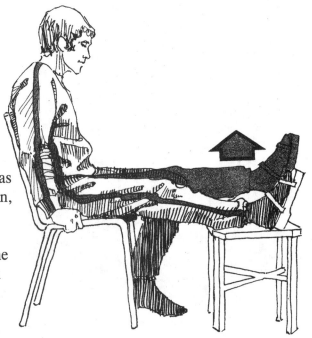

1. Sit on a chair and put your foot on a foot rest. Now, tighten the thigh muscles as hard as you can, then lift the weight, count three, lower the foot, and relax the muscles. Repeat three times.

2. Walk upstairs very slowly, counting three for each step. Come down the same way, counting three for each step. (You should feel the thigh muscles tighten up as they work.)

Do twenty steps and repeat three times.

Hamstring Muscles

Exercise the hamstring muscles very slowly and carefully so as not to pull and over-strain them. Play it safe and master the easy exercises before moving to the harder ones.

1. Stand up with your hands on your hips; then without bending your knees, touch the floor five times with the end of your fingers; then straighten up. Repeat three times.

2. Same exercise as (1), but touch the floor with your fists.

3. Same exercise as (1), but touch the floor with the palms of your hands.

4. Sit on the floor, put your hands behind your head, and touch your knees five times with your elbows. Repeat three times. (See page 27.)

5. Same as (4), but touch the floor with your elbows.

6. Same as (4) but touch your knees with your forehead.

7. Stand up and hold the backs of your legs with your hands, keeping your legs straight. Touch your knees five times with your forehead. Repeat three times. (See page 27.)

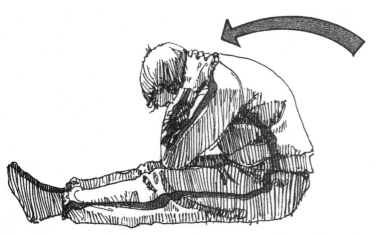

Hamstring Exercise 4

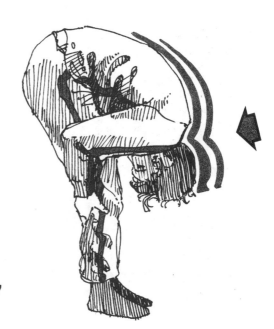

Hamstring Exercise 7

1. Lie on your back with your arms at your sides. Spread your legs as far as you can, sliding your heels on the floor. Repeat eight times.

2. Lie on your back with your arms at your sides. Spread your legs as far as you can and hook one foot around the foot of a bed. Now try to pull the bed towards you. Repeat three times.

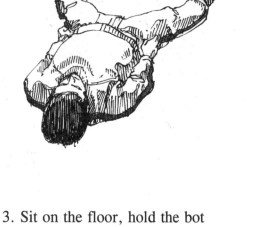

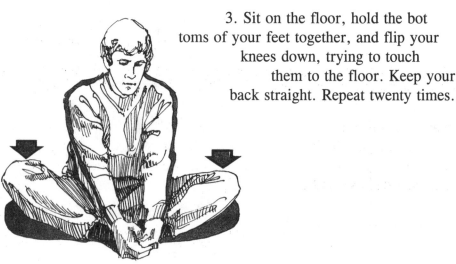

3. Sit on the floor, hold the bottoms of your feet together, and flip your knees down, trying to touch them to the floor. Keep your back straight. Repeat twenty times.

4. Stand up and try to do a split. Do not push too hard at the beginning but enough to feel the pressure on your groin. Hold your position for fifteen seconds and slide your feet back together to stand up. Repeating this exercise for five minutes every day will help you to make a complete split, like the ballet dancers do.

Ankles

Stand on your toes, then down onto the flat of your feet, then up on your toes again. If you have a long bar with a heavy weight, put it on your shoulders for better results. Repeat as often as you can for fifteen seconds.

ARMS

1. Do as many push-ups as you can within fifteen seconds. Repeat three times.

2. Using light weights (I work with twenty pounds):

(a) Stand up and lift your arms over your head (from the shoulders) as often as you can for fifteen seconds.

b) Stand up and extend your arms in front of you, from the shoulders, one at a time, as often as you can for fifteen seconds.

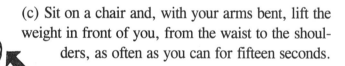

(c) Sit on a chair and, with your arms bent, lift the weight in front of you, from the waist to the shoulders, as often as you can for fifteen seconds.

HANDS

1. Squeeze a soft rubber ball as hard and as often as you can for fifteen seconds, then change hands.

2. Squeeze a spring as often as you can for fifteen seconds, then change hands.

WRISTS

1. Tie a weight at the end of a rope, and fasten the rope to a stick. Then rotate the weight on the stick as fast as you can for fifteen seconds. Extend your arms in front of you for better results.

2. Put your arm on a table, holding a light weight over the table edge for better handling. Then, lift the weight with the wrist only, not the arm. Repeat as often as you can for fifteen seconds.

WIND

A goaltender does not skate as much as the other players, but he often has periods of hard work, especially when his team plays a man short. I build up stamina for this by:

1. Riding a stationary bicycle at home with sprints of thirty seconds every two minutes. I start slowly the first few days, without the sprints, and do five miles. When I feel good, I start the sprints and increase the miles every day, up to twenty-five. My normal speed is twenty-eight m.p.h.

2. Running. I never liked running because of my asthma, but I recommend it — if you run, not jog. To obtain the best results, after you warm up, sprint as fast as you can for fifteen seconds, then walk back. Your pulse should beat normally by the time you come back to your starting point. You can repeat this exercise as often as you like. If you choose not to sprint, at least run at a fast pace. Do not jog, as jogging doesn't give your body enough exercise.

These exercises should take one hour of your time each day. Do them regularly and conscientiously and you will enjoy training camp. Try to report at your playing weight, even if some players say that you should have a few pounds to lose. The lighter you are, the faster you will regain your timing and the better you will play.

If you want to add speed to your conditioning, play tennis and ping-pong during the summer. These two sports will improve your reflexes, develop your coordination, and exercise the same muscles needed to play goal. Furthermore, they train your mind to always expect a return (a rebound in hockey).

Ping-pong adds more speed to your moves than tennis, because you are so close to the table. It speeds up communication between the eyes, brain, and hands or feet . . . so useful to a goaltender, when he has only a split second to make a save. Ping-pong will also improve your balance, because, as in hockey, you tilt the top of your body forward, keep your knees slightly bent, and stand still when you wait for the ball (a shot in hockey).

You face the ball and move sideways, not backward, to play it, just as you would move to stop a puck.

Some goalies move their feet and knees as the puck carrier approaches. They should remain still, as in ping-pong, face the shot, and stay at the edge of their goal-crease to cut down their angles. If they start back as the puck carrier comes closer to them, they give him the opening he needs for a shot.

When you wait for the ball in ping-pong, you don't stand with your feet together—you keep them apart the width of your shoulders for better balance—and that enables you to move more quickly. You use this same stance in the net, with just a small opening between your pads.

Never practice tennis, badminton, handball, or squash on a hard floor, as it is too hard on your legs.

The best way to improve your catching hand is to play catch. But if you play baseball, don't play in the infield. It's too dangerous for your fingers. The outfield position is much safer.

3 EQUIPMENT

Your goaltending can suffer if you don't wear the proper equipment or if you put it on the wrong way. Bulky equipment slows you down, and bad equipment is the cause of many injuries. As there is nothing worse than a bad bruise to put off your timing, let's see how we can prevent some of them.

ATHLETIC SUPPORT

When the athletic support moves out of place, you are uncomfortable and can be hurt when hit there. For better fit, wear the boxer type. The cup is bigger, stays in place more easily, and doesn't require cotton batting to cushion the shots. Don't use one with a sponge band in the midsection, as it will bother you when you bend forward.

UNDERWEAR

All goalies should wear long underwear to stay warm. Your timing will be off when you are cold. Furthermore, you should not take the chance of facing a hard shot when you are cold, for that is when they hurt you the most. Since you fear them, they often make you play poorly.

KNEEPADS

If the puck hits you often on the knee, wear knee pads. You will feel uncomfortable at first, but the added protection they give is well worth it. Hold them up with an elastic band below the knee. Don't use tape, as it won't stretch when your muscles expand, and it will exert an uncomfortable amount of pressure on the backs of your legs. For the same reason, use a garter belt to hold up your stockings.

LEG PADS

The leg pads should come to about three inches above the knee. If they don't, you'll be bit in the knee; then your game is very badly affected, since you will hardly be able to stand up to maintain your balance.

When the pads are too long, they affect your balance, your timing, and your moves, because they force you to play with your legs too far apart.

Make sure the bottoms of your pads cover the toes of your skates and almost touch the ice so you have a better chance to stop pucks shot along the ice.

If the puck often hits you on the inside of the leg, sew a piece of felt, one-half inch thick by four inches wide inside the pad, starting below the bottom strap, not the toe strap, to one inch above the knee strap.

*Extra padding
will help prevent injury
to the inside of the leg*

Fasten the toe strap behind the blade, not around it, so that the puck will not cut it when it hits the front of your blade. Check the toe strap before every game to make sure it is not partially cut or that the buckle is not broken. Too often a missing toe strap is not replaced, and when the goalie moves, the pad so often turns to the outside, leaving the leg unprotected against a bad blow on the shin.

It makes no difference whether the pads are old or new so long as they are long enough to protect well and stay in place.

Tie your pads so that the pressure from the straps on the back of your legs is very light. If you feel too much pressure when you crouch, your legs will tire more quickly and slow you down a split second toward the end of the game.

It takes about three weeks of daily practices to break in a new pair of pads. To break them in, buckle the bottom strap, not the toe strap under the foot, rather than behind the heel in the loop of the skate; this will give the pad the right curve on the top of the foot. This way, the straps do not hurt the backs of your legs and you will enjoy playing as you break in the new pads.

When the inside bottoms of your leg pads tend to lift up, keep them in place with a lace tied around the buckle of the side you want to pull back and back of the blade. Make sure not to pull the pad out of its natural position. If you do, it will touch the ice at times and make you slip. Buckle the bottom strap, not the toe strap, over the lace to keep it up and tight.

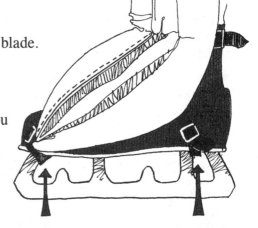

Correct positioning of the toe and bottom straps when playing

SHOULDER PADS

The arms are where the goalie is hit most, and these bruises usually hurt for a long time, as they are most often bone bruises. Yet most young goalies' arms are inadequately protected. We give them a couple of sleeves with very little padding (usually padded in the wrong place) that doesn't cushion enough of the blow, especially on hard shots.

Most shoulder pads protect only the outsides of both arms. Consequently, if you catch the puck with your left hand, the inside of your left arm is open, with no padding to cushion the shots. To correct this, sew pieces of felt, covered with fiber, inside the open arm, but not in the bend of the elbow, where you add a heavy sponge.

The shoulder pads are either too small or, more often, too large, leaving the neck area open and the shoulders unprotected. Furthermore, big shoulder pads slow the goalie down because of their extra bulk.

If you get hurt on the backhand arm or the tip of the shoulders, add pieces of felt and fibers there too.

ELBOW PADS

Elbow pads are not made for goaltenders. To solve this problem, you can sew a felt cushion on the shoulder pad. I never used elbow pads, but each time I hurt myself I wished I had.

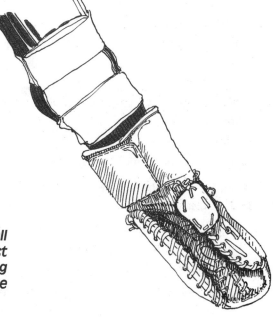

Use a basketball knee pad to protect your arms during practice

CHEST PROTECTOR

The chest protector should extend to the waist and must not be too thick. Choose one with flaps that protect the tips of your shoulders.

Wear it outside your pants. The habit of wearing it inside started years ago, when a rule change stated that no piece of equipment could show outside the sweater. The rule is still there, but today's smaller chest protectors can be worn outside the pants without showing. If you usually put yours inside your pants, try it outside; you'll feel much better—not so bulky in the mid-section.

The chest protector is there to protect the chest: when it's too long and hits the knees, it does not accomplish its purpose. The neck is then open and the high shots can hurt badly in that area. Furthermore, a chest protector that is too large requires a number of twists and knots in the back straps to make it fit, which can be very uncomfortable for the goalie.

CATCHING GLOVE

Leg pads, chest protector, and shoulder pads are a must to protect the goalie, but the catching glove—known as the bread and butter of the professional goalies—is his most important piece of equipment, Every goalie should have his own catching glove, It should have a big pocket so the goalie can not only catch the puck, but hold it. (Note to coaches: If your goalie's glove doesn't meet this requirement, try to change it for a better one; complain to playground authorities or team sponsors if necessary.)

Don't use a glove with a small pocket. The bigger it is, the easier it is to catch the puck. With a small pocket, the puck hits the palm of your hand and bounces out more often. Your glove can be too big for you and still be effective, but a small glove will always damage your game.

My glove has a fiber-covered sponge on the wrist and a molded fiber on the thumb to protect me against the hard shots. A shoe-maker can do that for you.

To break in a new glove, throw a lead ball at the bottom of the pocket where you normally catch the puck.

After using your glove, fold it around four pucks or a baseball and tie it with a rope or a lace, to protect the pocket when you put it in your bag.

To keep the leather soft and prevent it from cracking, oil your glove inside and outside once a month. Don't spare the oil, and don't forget to do the laces; if well oiled, they will last a long time.

BACK-HAND GLOVE

Most back-hand gloves have finger loops on the back piece. To get a better grasp on your stick, keep your fingers out of those loops, so that you hold the stick with your entire hand and not just the ends of your fingers.

Never bend the back piece of your glove to put the thick part of your stick on the ice. (I can do it with a straight back piece.) My back piece bends sometimes with the force of the pucks, but I never let it go too far.

WRIST BANDS

If you have no protector on your catching glove or if you get hurt by the puck with the one you have, use a wrist band (tennis band). Sew two of them together with a sponge in the middle and it will save you a lot of bruises.

I also use a plain wrist band on the back-hand side to prevent sweat from dripping into my glove.

HELMET

Choose one with good protection and which can be best adjusted to your mask. A helmet is not needed with the Jacques Plante mask, which covers all of the head, including the back.

TAPING FINGERS

If your fingers hurt when you catch the puck, tape them with white tape, leaving the knuckles open. I use cotton batting under the tape to better cushion the shots.

THE MASK

Wow! I almost forgot the mask, the most protective piece of equipment a goalie wears. The mask must provide both good protection and good visibility. I have seen many a goalie suffer a bad cut under his mask because it did not protect him enough. Some plastic masks should not be allowed on the market. The wired ones give more protection and although they cut down the visibility a little the kids can get used to them, as long as the mask isn't too big. Check to see if the bottom of the mask rests completely around the chin, not just at the end. If it does, the slightest move will make it drop under the chin and the wires will hit the mouth and cut the lips.

The Jacques Plante Mask

TURTLE NECK

A lot of players (including me) feel well only when their necks are warm. Some use a towel during practices, but a turtle neck is better and less bulky. You can buy them in sports stores and menswear stores.

STICK

Your choice of stick depends on your height, strength, and style. If the stick is too big and heavy you won't be able to use it to your advantage. If you are young, don't buy an adult-size stick, even though it may be of better quality. It will be too big for you and will hurt your game. (Note to coaches: Try to supply your goalie with the same model all the time so he does not lose his balance and puck-handling ability.)

The weight of your stick is most important. You must move very quickly against slap shots, and a heavy stick can slow your move long enough to cost you a goal. (It sometimes takes only half a second for the puck to go from the blue line to the goal.)

The lie of your stick influences your stance and your methods of stopping and handling the puck. If you are a stand-up goalie and like to handle the puck with your stick, use a low lie. A lie 14 or 15 will prevent you from recovering pucks rebounding away from you. You will then waste a split second moving closer to the puck in order to pass it to a teammate. A high lie makes you stand straighter, thus shifting your weight onto your heels at times, to offset your balance. Lie 10 and 11 can do the opposite by making you bring your weight onto your toes and lower your catching hand close to the ice, giving your opponents the chance to score in the top of the net and sometimes on the ice on your backhand side.

If you have trouble clearing the puck with your stick, practice doing it, changing from a high lie to a lower one or the other way around, until you feel comfortable.

The shape of the shoulders—square, round or sloped makes no difference, as long as the stick is well balanced and the length of the thick part suits your size and style. If you are short, a long thick part will make you play higher up and can hurt your balance. If you are tall and use a short thick part, you will crouch too much, and your balance will also be off.

Learn to hold your stick at the shoulder all the time so you are ready to make a save or prevent a pass. For a stronger grip, put one finger on top of the shoulder. This will help you control your stick better when you stop the puck or pass it with one hand.

Always wrap the same number of laps of tape around the knob of your stick (I use 25), to keep the same grip and help you when you handle the puck. Start taping your stick at about four inches below the shoulders so your fingers will not stick to the tape and make you feel uncomfortable.

Never cut the handle of your stick. You'll miss the extra length when you must poke the puck away or retrieve a rebound.

PANTS

There was a time when most goalies (including me) wore football-type pants, but now hockey pants are used. If you need extra protection inside your thighs to cushion the blows from the puck, cut the lining of your pants between the legs, slide in a piece of felt or hard sponge, then sew the opening closed.

SUSPENDERS

Buy heavy suspenders to hold your pants up. Do not use a rope or a belt. If your suspenders tend to slide off your shoulders, pull them together with a lace or a band especially made for that purpose. Wear your suspenders over your shoulder pads, but under the chest protector, which should be worn outside the pants.

SKATES

Your skates are essential to your balance as well as all your moves, so they must feel comfortable. Learn everything you can about them: What to buy, how to use them, how to sharpen them, etc. If they are too big or too small, your feet will tire fast and slow you down a split second, which could mean the difference between a save or a goal.

When you buy a pair of skates, always push the heel back to make sure you have the right size. A lot of players don't, only to complain about the bad fitting later on.

When you are young, buy skates the same size as your shoes, but later on, wear a size smaller. Tell the salesman whether you need a narrow or wide boot, as many of them do not know that skates vary in width.

If the bottoms of your feet get sore, a sponge insole often helps. You can find them in most drug stores and shoemaker's shops. I use them when my skates are new and a little too big for me. They give me a good fit and relax my feet.

Learn how to lace your skates—not too tight, not too loose. Since you stand in a crouch position most of the time, you add a lot of pressure on top of your feet and tire them more quickly when your skates are too tight, thus reducing your effectiveness by a split second.

If you get blisters on top of your ankles, put a sponge under the tongue of your skates until the skin toughens up. It's a good idea to protect yourself before you start hurting and use a sponge every time you begin skating in the fall.

In most cases, the skate sharpener or the trainer dulls off the skates for the goalies. You know how sharp you like your skates, so dull them off yourself. Pass the stone lightly along the edges of the blade, counting the number of times needed to obtain the right edge. (I pass the stone nine times on mine, Bernie Parent passes it six on his.)

To keep the edge longer, dry your skates after each use so that they don't rust.

Never leave your skates near a furnace or a radiator to dry as it will shrink the boot and dry the inside too much, which will hurt your feet.

To avoid unnecessary pain when the puck hits the end of your boot, keep your big toenails short. Do the same for your finger-nails.

HOW TO LOOK AFTER YOUR EQUIPMENT

You wear so much equipment (about forty pounds of it) that it should fit you well and offer the right protection. After you find what you need, take good care of it to keep it as long as possible and enjoy wearing it.

The equipment is expensive and hard to break in, so it represents an investment of both money and time. Protect that investment.

After using the equipment, hang it to dry, then check it over before putting it in your bag. It takes only a few minutes, but it's time well spent.

Skates

Are they sharp enough for the next game? Are all the rivets in place and tight enough? Are the laces still good?

Catching Glove

Are the laces of the pocket still good? Is the leather loop inside the glove still there to hold the fingers? How are the laces on the cuff? Don't play without them.

Back-hand Glove

Do you have laces on the cuff? Are they good enough? How is the palm? If there are big holes in it, a splinter in your stick can hurt you badly. You can replace the palm in a minute, and use your glove immediately, as if you had had it for a year. Consult a sporting goods store for information on this.

Shoulder Pads

How are the laces in front and back? Do the pads protect you properly? If not, sew some felt where it hurts.

Mask

How are the straps? Is there enough elasticity in them? If not, change them right away so the mask will stay in place. Is the mask cracked? If so, don't play with it. Think of what could happen if you were hit—it could be worse than playing without one.

Athletic Support

Is the elastic still good at the waist and between the legs? If not, change it for better comfort and protection. Is the cup still good? Check to see that it is not cracked.

Pants

Are the fibers in the thighs broken? If you push hard enough with your thumbs, you can easily find a cracked fiber.

Do you have all the buttons to hold on the braces?

Are the braces still good enough to hold the pants up? How are the snaps that keep the braces at the right length?

Garter Belt

How are the loops that hold the stockings? If they give way often, buy a new garter belt, because this problem can't be fixed.

Pads

Is the leather at the bottom holding on, or is the padding coming out through a hole?

Are the toe and back straps cut? If so, replace them.

Is the toe strap holding on firmly enough to the pad? If not, sew it on.

How are the buckles holding the toe strap? Are they broken or bent?

Lace Holding the Pad in Place

If you use a lace to hold the inside of your pad in place, check to see if it is worn. If it is, cover the weak spot with white tape. You don't have to change the lace every time, because one practice can wear it out.

If any of your equipment needs repair, do it before packing your bag or you'll forget, and the equipment will go from bad to worse. You'll play badly, get hurt more often, and quickly wear out the equipment.

No one will fix it unless you do it yourself or, if the team owns the equipment, tell your trainer. In this case, tell the trainer right after practice, not just before the next one, so be has time to have it repaired.

When you pack your bag, don't just throw in your equipment. Lay it neatly in place. Fold your gloves correctly and put them on top of the chest protector at the bottom of the bag. Then the shoulder pads, the smaller pieces, and the pants. Put your mask in the leg of your pants. The skates go in last. Always pack your bag the same way so you won't leave out any piece of equipment. Use a big enough bag. It costs a few dollars more, but it's well worth it to protect your equipment

Keeping an eye on the puck during action from close in

4 HOW TO PLAY GOAL

Playing goal can be a lot of fun when you "let the puck play you" instead of "you, playing the puck." This means: Block your angles well.

Don't catch the puck on your backhand side; use your backhand glove.

Don't stop the puck with your skate on your forehand side instead of your stick. Don't try to catch every low shot, but use your stick or your pad whenever you can.

Help yourself to play goal the easy way—the *easier* way—by learning now *how to let the puck play you.*

SKATING

You will never be a good goalie unless you learn to skate as well as the forwards, so you can stop the puck more easily or race after it outside your net. It isn't easy to skate while wearing all your bulky, heavy goaltending equipment. Those broad leg pads force your legs far apart, thus changing your stride completely, and they'll make a bad skater worse.

Goaltenders need special skating exercises, because they usually take only two or three quick strides to poke the puck away from an opponent, or stop it, or pass it to a teammate. They must be able to pivot on themselves to regain their net in a hurry and do so while skating backward or sideways.

Practice starting quickly, taking a few strides, stopping on the outside skate, and skating backward, as you would in a game.

Stopping on the outside foot is very important. A goalie never stops on the inside one, for it means turning away from the puck for the split second that may mean a goal.

Practice skating forward, stopping on the outside foot, then skating backward

Practice stopping on both the left and right foot

Even when the goalie moves back and forth across the goal line to follow the puck, he stops on the outside foot as he puts it against the goal post. When a puck carrier cuts in front of the net, again, the goalie stops on the outside foot after he makes a save. If he didn't, how could he retain his balance and be ready for a rebound?

Stopping the puck behind the net is not as easy as it looks. The goalie must know how to pivot, on both sides, out of his net. It must be done in a split second and only practice can give you that ability.

HOW TO STAND IN THE NET

You will always have trouble stopping the puck if you don't stand up properly and retain your balance. For good balance, keep your weight on the balls of your feet with the inside of your back-hand glove touching the outside top of your pad and your catching glove resting knee high, barely touching the outside of your pad.

If your catching glove is lower, your weight transfers to your toes, weakening your defense against shots along the ice on your stick side and at the top on your glove side.

If your catching glove is above your knee, your weight is on your heels and you'll be weak at the bottom of the net on both sides.

Keep the top of your body tilted forward to move toward the puck carrier, not backward into the net. When you go backwards, you transfer your weight to your heels, giving yourself a lot of problems against low shots inside the goal posts.

On a *straight shot,* stand at the edge of the goal crease with the backs of your skates resting on the line, to deflect the puck behind the goal line. When you play back, the rebound stays in front of the goal line, where an opponent can pick it up to score.

When the puck can be deflected by an opponent standing few feet

How to stand in the net

in front of you, move right behind him and watch his stick. But remember also to play the puck in case it is not deflected.

In a scramble in front of the net or a shot from close in with a player half screening you, play the puck on the side where you can see it all the way. If the opponent shoots across your team-mate to the other side, chances are very good that your teammate will stop the puck.

Why is it so hard to stop a *player coming on his wrong wing*? It's very simple; most goalies line themselves up with the player, not the puck, and forget that the stick is about five feet further on the open side.

**Play the puck on the side where
you can see it all the way**

Always line yourself up with the middle of the stick on straight shots and with the puck on angle shots. At first you'll find it hard, but the results should convince you that this is the only way to play a player coming in on the wrong wing.

On a breakaway or a penalty shot, stay at the edge of your goal crease, with the front of your skates on the line, and wait for the puck carrier to make the first move. Line yourself up with the middle of his stick, and play every player for a shot. But at the same time, say to yourself, "If the player tries to deke me, most of the time he'll go to his backhand." Remember the players who tend to deke on their forehands, and play them accordingly.

Stand up on the breakaway to recover the rebounds or follow the players trying to deke you. On penalty shots, the players are so nervous that they usually shoot. Since there is no rebound to worry about, you can hit the ice but not too soon.

On a corner face-off, always be ready to make a save when the opposing centerman faces you. Stand on the corner of your goal crease, never against the goal line, where you give a big opening to your opponent.

On a corner face-off, make sure you can see the slot man's stick, in case the puck goes to him for a slap shot. Talk with your teammates before each face-off, especially the center man, and remind him to be more careful when his opponent faces the net with his forehand. In this case, your centerman should never draw the puck toward you.

When the puck is behind the goal line, always keep one skate against the goal post and the other one on the goal line, not in front, so the puck will not hit you and bounce into the net.

When the puck slides back and forth in front of the net, remain at the edge of your goal crease, with the front of your skate on the line. Watch who handles the puck—a hard shooter? a playmaker?—and adjust your moves with each one. Crouch a little more

When a player cuts 15 feet in front of the net, move toward him and in the same direction as he is skating.

Wrong! **The goalie's stick is too far away and he's sitting on his heels; for proper stance, see page 51.**

than usual so you won't be caught off balance on a quick pass or a deflection. Always keep your stick on the ice, and hold it at the shoulders.

When a player cuts fifteen feet in front of the net, you cannot poke the puck away from him, so move toward him and in the same direction as he is skating. This will force him away from you and, because he is skating away from the net, reduce his shooting capability. As you move, push gently with the back foot, as far as you have to, to cover your angles. Hold your stick at the shoulders and keep it on the ice. Bend your knees a little, and drop your back leg to the ice when the player shoots. Use your backhand glove and elbow on high shots. If you drop your leg too soon, you won't go out as far as you should and your shoulder, not your chest, will face the puck.

The hardest save to make is against a player cutting in front of the net on his *backhand*, because he can lift the puck sharply on your short side, slide it on the ice on either side, carry it across the goal mouth, or slide it between your legs as you follow him.

More bad goals are scored on *backhand shots* than on any others, because the goalies don't get enough experience with them, fear the high shots, and tend to lift up. To overcome this problem, stand outside your goal crease and bring your shoulders in. This will help you keep your stick on the ice and force you to face the puck rather than back away from it. If the puck carrier tries to deke you, poke the puck away from him. If he shoots you'll be ready.

The *high backhand shots* will not bother you either if you stand outside your goal crease, because there won't be any room at the top of the net.

HOW TO SLIDE ACROSS THE GOAL LINE

When the puck is behind the goal line, the best way to move from one goal post to the other is to slide the front skate sideways and rest it on the far post, all in one move.

This way, you can send your stick ahead of you to the outside of the goal post to prevent a pass, and your body will be facing the front of the net, in position to make a save if a pass is completed to the front of the net.

If you turn your front skate, you cannot send your stick ahead of you to prevent a pass. You lose a split second in putting the heel of your skate against the goal post. If a pass is completed to the front of the net, your body is facing the goal post, and the split second you need to regain your defensive position is often too long to prevent a goal.

These moves will become routine only after you become a good skater and can skate forward and backward and can pivot and turn like a figure skater.

Sliding across goal mouth with skate sideways

Stick positioned to prevent pass from behind

**Make sure
that your
skate rests
snugly against
the goal post**

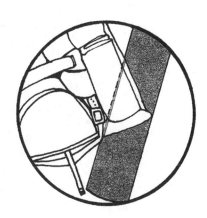

The best exercise is to change from forward skating to backward, to forward, to backward, taking only a couple of strides between each turn, and turning left and right.

To improve your stability and balance, do some stop-and-start skating between one blue line and the red line. Stop on the inside foot at one end and the outside foot at the other end. You must switch between right and left in this exercise also. Don't always stop on the inside of the same foot just because you have trouble on the other one. On the contrary, practice the weak side more.

HOW TO USE YOUR CATCHING GLOVE

Don't try to catch everything you can lay your hand on. If you do, you will crouch too much, anticipate plays, be off balance, tend to play back in your net, give a lot of rebounds, and leave a big opening for your opponents.

Try to catch the puck in mid-air, not against your chest, to control it faster and pass it to a teammate sooner. The split second you need to control the puck after it hits your chest is often long enough to force you to hold it for a face-off.

Catch the puck in mid-air, with the back-hand glove behind the catching glove

When you catch the puck above the waist and in front of you, if possible put your backhand glove behind the catching glove, to protect yourself in case you miss the puck at the last moment. Don't forget to hold your stick at the shoulders, ready to pass the puck as soon as you put it on the ice.

Catch every puck you can on your glove side, even the ones over or beside the net, to control it and do what you want with it. When you let the puck hit the boards or the glass, you never know where it will bounce or who will pick it up on the rebound. So why not catch it?

When you catch the puck and want a face-off, bring your catching glove to your body to prevent an opponent from hitting the puck away from you. Then drop to your knees to avoid being hit yourself.

HOW TO FREEZE THE PUCK WITH YOUR GLOVE

When you hold the puck on the ice with your catching glove, lay the thick part of your stick in front of your glove, not behind it, to prevent an opponent from poking it away from you.

THE STICK AND HOW TO USE IT

Your stick will be a lifesaver if you choose the right one for you and learn how to poke the puck away from an opponent crossing in front of you . . . how to deflect the puck to a corner of the rink … how to pass the puck to a teammate . . . how to kill a rebound, etc.

When the puck is in your zone always hold your stick at the shoulders, with one finger on top to keep the proper balance so you can use it in a split second. When you hold your stick at the handle, you waste time in shifting your grip to the shoulder and you'll often miss an easy save.

On a long shot, you want to control the puck after a stick save. Place the stick against your pad, not the end of your skate, to cushion the rebound. If you have time, put your catching glove behind your stick for better results.

When you make a stick save with a lot of players around you, do not stop the puck before passing it to the corner. Turn your stick and steer the puck to the corner in one motion to avoid a rebound or losing it to an opponent. When you steer the puck to a corner of the rink, try to send it in the same direction it came from to prevent a rebound in front of the goal line.

Be very careful when you stop the puck on your stick side, because the heel of your stick lifts up when you play a shot away from your body. Always be ready to use your skate on that side.

Practice stopping the puck in the air on your backhand side with the thick part of your stick until you succeed three times out of five. Hold your stick with one finger on top of the shoulders to control it better and prevent it from turning in your hand when the puck hits the blade or the inside of the thick part.

This practice comes in handy when the puck is shot from close in, about two feet away from you.

Practice passing the puck to your left and your right, holding your stick with only one hand. This will help you clear the puck faster after you make a save or when a loose puck comes near you.

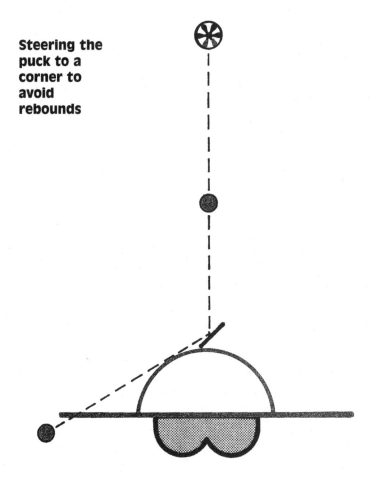

Steering the puck to a corner to avoid rebounds

Using two hands on your stick is also very important and can get you out of a lot of tight spots. Learn to handle the puck with two hands on your stick and keep your gloves on. Too many goaltenders take them off when their coach calls for a passing exercise.

When you are expecting a shot, hold your stick at an angle to the puck, not resting it at the end of your skates, so you will deflect the puck to the side of the net, not to the front. When you hold your stick at the end of your skates, your elbow is away and in front of you, and you will seldom have time to bring it in against your body to stop a waist-high puck shot from close in.

Don't kick your stick with your skate to clear the puck. This move will cause too many rebounds, and if you kick too soon, the puck will slide under your stick. However, if an opponent is standing just in front of you and there is no chance to prevent him from taking the rebound after you make a save, you can kick the puck away.

When you are expecting a shot, always leave your stick on the ice so you can move quickly on all possible deflections. You'll save a split second to stop the puck and allow yourself more strength against the hard shots along the ice. If you keep your stick on the ice, you will notice how many saves you make on screen shots or deflections with very little effort.

When your stick is off the ice, the puck often slides under it before you can react. Furthermore, with your stick off the ice you stand up straighter, often transfer your weight to your heels, and thus reduce your effectiveness on low shots.

When you move across the goal line to follow an opponent carrying the puck behind the net, always send your stick ahead of you to the outside of the goal post to prevent a pass to the front. Hold your stick at the shoulders and put only the blade, not the thick part, on the ice. This way your body faces the front of the net and you will save a split second to regain your defensive position if the pass is completed.

Moving the blade of your stick outside the goal post when an opponent moves swiftly 'round the back of the net isn't easy to do. If you wait until you have rested your skate against the post, you may be too late to prevent the pass to the front.

The stick must move in a half circle and stop with the glove outside the post to put the blade on the goal line an prevent the puck

Practice moving across the goal line, sending the stick ahead of you in a sweeping motion

from hitting it and deflecting into the net. If you keep your wrist and the forearm straight, with the stick handle glued to your elbow, you can easily execute this move. The handle will automatically go behind your back, not outside the net. However, it won't work if you put your legs together when you stop or keep your back leg to the rear of the net instead of on the goal line.

If the opponent keeps the puck and goes to the corner of the rink, put the handle of the stick outside the net to prevent a pass behind you. Some goaltenders have objected that, in putting the blade and the glove outside the post, they leave an opening of about one foot near the post. That's true, but when an opponent moves 'round behind the net, he very seldom passes the puck there.

Practice this move without moving your feet and keep your skate against the post. When you master the sweeping in a half-circle without hooking the handle on the horizontal bar or putting it outside the post, start sliding from one side to the other. If it then becomes harder to put the stick and glove in place than when you stand still, you are controlling your stick the wrong way or your feet are not in the right position.

On screen shots from the blue line, look for the puck between the players' legs, not over their shoulders. Hold your stick at the shoulders, with the thick part near the ice, (1) to stop the pucks shot on the ice; (2) to cover more room than you can with only the blade; (3) to play deflections better and to freeze the puck more easily after a save. Using only the blade, you allow a lot of rebounds, and it is more difficult to freeze the puck after a save.

Never take a stick save for granted, even if the puck is sliding very slowly. It can always jump over a piece of ice and into the net. Protect yourself and put your catching glove or your pads behind your stick.

HOW TO STOP THE PUCK BEHIND THE GOAL

Stopping the puck behind the net is not as easy as it looks. It won't be too difficult, though, if the goalie knows how to pivot on both sides, out of his net, and come back just as fast to make room for a teammate skating in to pick up the puck or to get away from an opponent trying to interfere with him.

When you are just beginning to play goal, go behind the net only when the puck is shot from outside the blue line. This will give you plenty of time to get to the puck and come back before an opponent is close to you.

Later on, as you gain speed and confidence, you'll be able to go behind the net when the shooter is inside the blue line; but then, you must be very fast and know in advance what to do with the

Stopping the puck behind the goal (1)

puck, since there is always a possibility of an opponent racing toward you or even standing behind the net, waiting for the puck. If you know he is there, pass the puck back to the corner it came from, expect to be hit or pushed, but do not let him hold you behind the net. You must regain your goal at all costs.

When a goalie stops the puck behind his net, he must leave it about six inches from the boards so that his teammate can pick it up easily without danger of being checked by an opponent.

Learn to stop the puck behind the net while holding your stick at the shoulder with one hand. This will give you a chance to reach out farther and allows you a split second more to regain your net. Use the blade, not the thick part of your stick, so that if you have to return the puck to the corner you won't waste time.

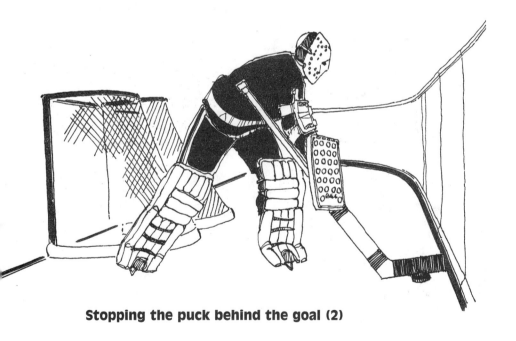

Stopping the puck behind the goal (2)

WHERE TO PASS THE PUCK

When the goalie sees that an opponent will pick up the puck if he leaves it behind his net, he must always pass it to the corner of the rink it came from, not behind him.

If you have time to pass the puck on your forehand, use two hands on the stick. One hand can be used easily on the backhand side.

HOW TO PREVENT A PASS FROM BEHIND THE NET

When an opponent handles the puck behind the net, keep the blade of your stick, not the thick part, outside the goal post and behind the goal line to prevent a possible pass to the front, and to be ready for a save if the pass is completed.

When you put all your stick on the ice you lose a split second when you straighten up to regain your defensive position if the pass is completed to the front of the net.

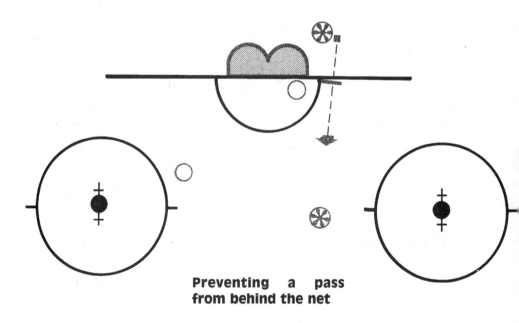

Preventing a pass from behind the net

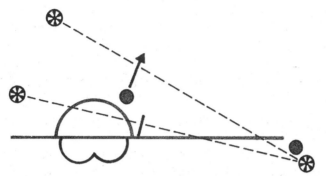

Playing a corner pass from behind the goal line

HOW TO PLAY A CORNER PASS COMING FROM BEHIND THE GOAL LINE

When a pass goes from behind the goal line across the goal mouth, the puck belongs to you, while your defense watches the slot man standing about twenty feet in front of the net. On this play, hold your stick at the shoulders, keep your skate on the goal post, face the front of the net, and be ready to use your stick to intercept the puck if it is passed along the ice. Holding your stick at the shoulders will give you a good grip on it so you can stop the pass. After you do, leave the puck at your side for a teammate or freeze it for a face-off if there is danger. If you freeze it, put your catching glove on the puck and place the thick part of your stick in front of the puck to protect it.

HOW TO POKE THE PUCK AWAY FROM AN OPPONENT

When you reach out to poke the puck away from an opponent crossing in front of you, wait until he is almost even with the net before making your move, and play the puck with the bottom of your blade. If you hook the puck with the top of your blade, there is a chance that the puck will follow the handle and slide toward you for a goal.

Do not hold your stick back for fear of tripping the puck carrier. If you do, he will often have enough room to pull back and beat you.

Make sure the stick faces center ice, not the side boards, when you reach out after the puck. If you do not, a clever opponent will often have enough time to pull away from you or stop to score on the short side.

Poking the puck away from an opponent

When you reach out on this play, always drop your back knee to the ice to protect yourself against a possible shot on the short side or between your legs.

To poke the puck away from a player cutting in front of the goal, throw your stick forward in a very aggressive move, holding the handle at the very end and holding your stretched-out position

But first, you must have absolute confidence in your ability to force your opponent to cut in front of the net, rather than go to the short side. To succeed, slide your hand about four inches above the stick shoulders, in position to attack. This attack must be like a snake striking, not allowing the enemy time to react.

This move is best done when the goaltender throws himself on his knees as he sends his stick toward the center of the ice. The leg on the short side of the post remains straight out behind you, to protect the short side.

If one of your knees stays up as you play the puck, it hits your stomach and shortens your reach by about two feet . . . enough room for the puck carrier to deke you. You should be able to stretch your stick as far as two small lines painted between the face-off circles.

All these moves will be useless if you cannot put your stick flat on the ice. To succeed move the back of your glove out of the way and turn your fingers, so they do not touch the ice

Remember: (1) keep the heel of your stick facing the puck; (2) slide the hand from the shoulders to the end of the handle. (3) move forward while dropping your front knee to the ice; (4) don't try to poke the puck away from an opponent coming straight at you.

HOW TO PLAY THE ANGLES

To cover your angles better, guide yourself by the indications already painted on the ice: the face-off circles in the corners of the rink, at the blue line, and at center ice, plus the ends of the blue lines near the boards.

Play at the edge of the goal crease, with the back of your skates resting on the line, not the front, to cover the angles better and cut down the size of the opening for your opponent.

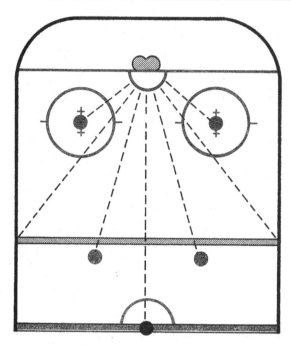

On an angle shot from your left (with the puck in line with the face-off circle), put your right foot on the corner of your goal crease. If the puck is in line with the corner of the cross in the face-off circle, stand with the corner of the goal crease between your feet. If the shooter tries to cross in front of the net, never move backwards, move across the outside of the goal crease.

If the puck carrier is a hard shooter, come out a little past the edge of your goal crease. But if the puck is sliding all over in your end, with a lot of opponents buzzing around the net, stay inside the crease.

When your defenseman forces the puck carrier to shoot from an angle, come out as far as you want and face the puck. Move out slowly to keep your stick on the ice and be ready for the shot. Some opponents shoot sooner than others, or from the wrong foot, and will catch you off balance if you come out too fast.

Cover your angles better by moving out so that the heel of your skate is on the goal crease

Always stand up on an angle save or on a rebound from one. Too many goalies, even in the pro leagues, drop one knee to the ice on those shots, opening a hole at the top of the net and between their legs. Furthermore, dropping to one knee puts them at a disadvantage if their opponent decides to deke them. You cover more room standing up, control the rebounds more easily, and can react faster if the player tries to deke you. But it's very hard to get used to standing up, especially on the rebounds. You'll have to remind yourself every time you fall down.

TWO-ON-ONE

On a two-on-one breakaway, the puck and the puck carrier belong to the goalie. So stay at the edge of your goal crease, even when he comes close to you. Don't worry about the pass, which belongs to your defenseman. If you move back and anticipate a pass, and the player shoots for a goal, you will be held responsible. You must have faith in your defenseman as he must have faith in you. Establish this system during practices and it should work most of the time.

It will not work when your defenseman plays too much of the middle and lets the puck carrier deke you. The pass belongs to the defenseman, but he must also prevent the puck carrier from crossing in front of the net. When it comes to this point, the defenseman has no choice and must play the puck carrier, hoping the pass will not be completed to the open man.

On these one-on-one, three-on-one, or two-on-three breakaways, the goalie must yell at his defensemen and remind them what to do.

Reaching as far as you can to make a fantastic catch or a great skate save really means that you were caught off balance or out of position or did not cover your angles properly. When you play the right way, you can stop everything without moving more than one foot either way, except on a pass across the net, a rebound, or a deflection. When this happens, study your position and try to find out what you did wrong,

COVER ANGLES EVENLY

Never leave a big opening on your catching glove side in hope that the puck carrier will shoot for it. If you do, you'll have to move before the shot and miss many hard ones.

The good players will soon learn your style and beat you on your short side. Although some nights you'll be red hot, on others, you'll be not so hot — when you guess wrong.

Usually, a goalie gives a big hole on his glove side because of a weak back-hand. Instead of correcting a weakness by a mistake, why not improve the weak side and enjoy playing goal the right way.

HOW TO FOLLOW THE PUCK

Your job is to stop the puck, so never take your eyes off it — even when the play is at the other end of the rink. Goals have been scored from there because some goalies were daydreaming or looking up in the stands.

When the puck is *behind your net*, follow it out of the corner of your eye. Hold your stick at the shoulders, with the blade outside the goal post, to prevent a pass to the front. Your chest will then face the front of the net and you will be in position to make a save if the pass is completed.

Never face the back of the net. If a pass should be completed, the time you need to regain your defensive position will often be too long for you to prevent a goal.

When an opponent with a *hard shot* handles the puck at the blue line, move out further to block your angles. Hold your stick at the shoulders and on the ice, to keep your balance and be ready for a deflection.

On screen shots from the blue line, follow the puck between the players' legs, not over their shoulders. Hold your stick at the shoulders, with the thick part almost touching the ice. If the shot is off the ice, stop it with your backhand glove, not your pads, to control the puck better. Catch all the pucks you can on these shots, so your opponents won't have a chance to poke the rebound into the net. If you cannot pass the puck to a teammate, hold it for a face-off, drop to your knees, and bring your catching glove to your stomach.

On a screen shot from close in, play the top of the net when your teammate falls down to make a save. Hold your stick at the shoulders and keep it on the ice, in case the puck slides past your teammate.

If your teammate *stands up*, crouch down and follow the puck

On screen shots,
follow the puck
between the
player's leg (1).

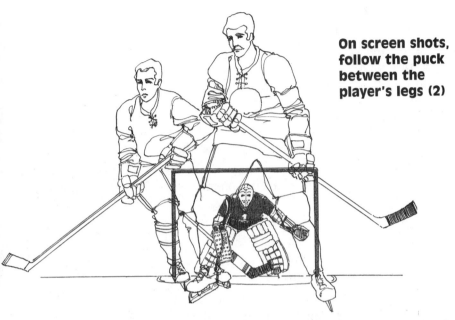

On screen shots, follow the puck between the player's legs (2)

from the side directly in line with you. If the shot goes to the far side there's a good chance your man will Stop it.

Always be prepared for a shot on the net when an opponent controls the puck, *even from a very bad angle.* Play the puck and forget the pass, which belongs to your teammate standing in front of the net. If you anticipate a pass and turn your body toward the open man, you will let in some bad goals from those impossible angles. Remember that your chest should always face the puck when it is in front of the goal line.

When the puck is behind the goal line, the open man standing beside the net belongs to you. Your defenseman takes the one in the slot. To check him, he should stand about a stick's length away from your crease, not in it, to play the pass to the slot instead of behind you. When he is too close, tell him to move back and give you ten feet. Again, hold your stick at the shoulders, to be in your defensive position if the pass is completed to the front.

On a breakaway, *always look at the puck*, not at the player's eyes. Look at the eyes only when you are lying on the ice and cannot get up in time to make a save. Then you might be able to guess where the player will shoot and be lucky enough to make a save by lifting a leg, a hand, or your stick.

HOW TO HANDLE THE PUCK

If you want to save yourself some work and enjoy playing more, you must learn how to go out of your net after the puck... every time you can get it before an opponent can or help a teammate control it faster.

When to pass

When the puck is shot around the boards from outside the blue line, stop it and leave it about six inches from the boards. Do not leave it against the boards or on the back of the net, because your teammate could be checked while trying to control it. On this play, hold your stick at the shoulders with one hand so you can reach farther and gain a split second for the return to your net.

If you hold your stick with two hands, you'll have to get closer to the boards and you'll waste time stopping the puck. If you linger too long, you may interfere with your teammate or give an opponent a chance to hit you.

When the puck is shot from outside the blue line, you should have plenty of time to stop it and regain your net. But from inside the blue line, you have to move very fast. Be very careful and never leave the puck behind the net. Everything has to be done in a split second: Going out after the puck, passing it back where it came from, and returning to your net. This is an anticipation play and a risky one. If you miss the puck or you are checked before controlling it, it will often cost you a goal. But don't worry about it, as long as it doesn't happen too often. (It happened to me six times between 1943 and 1972.)

You will tend to leave the net more often when your team is playing badly, because the puck will be in your end more often. Be very careful then, especially if there are opponents nearby. You will be more tired than usual; you'll move more slowly and get hit more.

When to leave puck

When you stop the puck behind your net and see that an opponent will pick it up if you leave it there, always return it to the corner it came from—not behind the net, where you cannot see what is happening. If a teammate yells for it, ignore him, because an opponent may anticipate your pass, intercept the puck, and score before you can regain your net.

When you control the puck near your net, leave it beside the net, not behind it, to let your teammate go where he wants, If you put the puck behind the net your teammate will have no chance to outwit his opponent.

When to poke puck

When the puck lands beside your net after a rebound or coming off the boards, do not let your teammate handle it when an opponent is right behind him. If you do, he will often be hit before he can bring it under control and he will lose it. To prevent this, poke the puck away just as your teammate goes to pick it up. He will then skate behind the net with his pursuer but the puck will be out of the danger zone. If you establish this system with your teammates, they'll appreciate it. You'll save them a lot of bruises and make their job much easier. But if your teammate thinks he can handle the puck and tells you to leave it there, don't touch it. Be on your toes, though, in case he is checked and loses the puck.

Rebound off boards

Train your mind to play the rebounds off the boards after the puck misses the net. When the puck bounces back in front, push it to

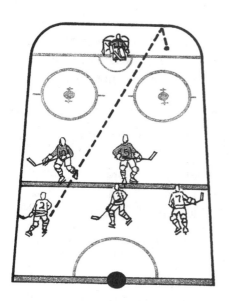

Playing rebounds from shots outside the blue line

the corner of the rink as soon as you touch it or leave it beside your net for your man. *Hold your stick at the shoulders and stop the rebound with one hand on your stick. Face the front of the net and be ready for a save if the puck bounces over your stick.*

When the puck is shot from outside the blue line to the opposite corner of the rink, lively boards can make it bounce back in front of the goal line. When that happens, race out toward the corner as soon as the puck is shot, play the rebound off the boards, and shoot it back at the boards. Go as close to the puck as you have to. If you fear being trapped and stop halfway, you'll miss the puck and have a lot of problems. After you play the puck, move out of the way as fast as you can to avoid being bit by the opponent charging in.

On the same corner shots, when the puck bounces and is not safe to play with your stick, pick it up with your glove and hold it for a face-off. You are allowed to, since you are in front of the goal line.

Tell him you are passing

When you control the puck, do not hesitate to pass it to a teammate if you can help him to counter-attack faster. If you leave it near your net and wait for him to pick it up, an opponent can move in and check him.

When you want to pass the puck to a teammate, tell him you are doing it. Then he won't skate away from you but expect your pass and be ready for it. A goalie cannot afford to make a mistake when he controls the puck. That is why it is very important for him to know, before he touches the puck, what he is going to do with it!

Keep feet still

Be very careful not to move your leg forward and give rebounds with your pad, especially on angle shots. I'm not talking of kicking the puck, but only moving the leg forward. Keep your knees bent and the puck will drop at your feet and you'll be able to clear it with your stick as soon as it touches the ice.

Kick the puck only when an opponent stands beside you, waiting for the rebound.

Stop the puck with your skate on the stick side only on long shots, on a shot from a pass across the net, or when a player tries to deke you—never on a close-in shot. On this shot, the stick is faster and your pads face the puck to cover a larger area.

When an opponent is standing in the line of the puck, waiting for the rebound, turn your foot so the puck dies on your blade and freeze it with your catching glove. This is very hard to do, and requires a lot of practice. Most goalies never master it, because they drop their back knee to the ice.

A full split on long shots means that the goalie was caught off balance or played too far back into his net, leaving a big opening he couldn't cover with his stick. It looks like a fantastic save, but if you analyze your position, you'll find you were too far back and should have been more careful to cover your angles. These desperate saves will happen less and less often as you gain experience.

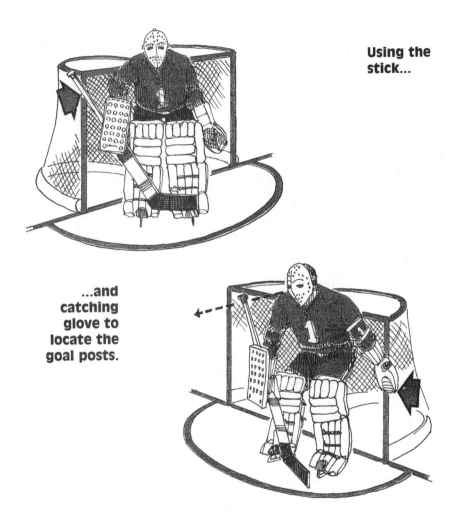

Using the stick...

...and catching glove to locate the goal posts.

HOW TO REGAIN YOUR NET

When you are returning to your net you must be able to move into position without taking your eyes off the puck. You do this by locating the goal posts by touch—with the handle of your stick on one side and your catching glove on the other. As soon as you are back in your net make sure you put your skate against the post and keep it there as long as the puck is behind the goal line. Hold your stick at the shoulders.

HOW TO PLAY A BLOOPER

Bloopers are very easy to play if you don't let the puck drop in front of you. Move out when a player takes his position to flip the puck and catch it before it hits the ice. If it falls short and bounces by you when you are far enough in front of the net, it will also miss the net. It will be a goal if you wait for it in your net.

When the puck bounces on the ice do not try to control it with your stick. Stand behind the puck and catch it for a face-off. If you bring a blooper under control, you can pass it to a teammate. However, your man must be standing against the boards; if you pass to the middle of the rink, an opponent can intercept it and move in before you regain your goal.

HOW TO PREVENT REBOUNDS

It is very important to control rebounds after every shot on the net. Learn to keep the puck at your feet and pass it to a teammate, when you can. Try to plan what you will do with the puck if you get it, because in most cases you will only have a split second to handle it.

To give fewer rebounds on close shots and more easily control your balance, hold your weight on the stick side, with the other leg a little behind. This keeps your pads together at the top and leaves only a small opening at the bottom. On low shots on the catching glove side, stretch the leg sideways to make a save. Your stick covers the shots on the ice, between the legs and the backhand side. This stance also helps you to keep your feet still, prevents you from shifting your weight too soon on a breakaway, and indirectly forces the puck carrier to make the first move.

Where to hold your stick

Hold your stick against the bottoms of your pads, not the ends of your skates, to soften the shots and kill the rebounds.

The basic stance to prevent rebounds

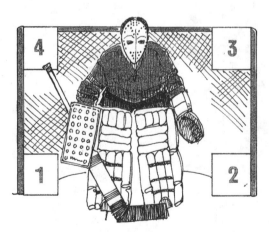

**The strong pôints of a goaltender: 2 and 4;
the weak points: 1 and 3.**

From the basic position you can easily shift to the right or left.

When you expect a shot, hold the blade of your stick away from your feet, in a 45-degree angle to the trajectory of the puck, to send it away from the net, not in front. Never hold your stick 'way out in front of you. This shifts your weight to your toes and slows you down on low shots. A lot of shots will also beat you between the legs before you can react.

Use your back-hand glove to make a save on that side. It is faster and safer than reaching with the catching glove. Learn to turn your wrist down to drop the puck at your feet. Hold your stick at the shoulders so you can clear the puck away in one motion, as soon as it hits the ice.

Learn to poke the puck away with your back-hand glove when an opponent is close by or to let your teammate handle the rebound.

WHY STAND UP?

A stand-up goalie should have more success than the ones who are always falling to the ice. If he covers his angles well he can control and recover many rebounds the others miss; a flopping goalie is often beaten on high shots and rebounds. When you stand up and cover your angles well, your opponents cannot see much to shoot for, but if you play on your knees, they will shoot for the opening you create when you fall down. So stand up! You'll tire less and play better.

WHY AND HOW TO TALK TO THE PLAYERS

Only part of the goalie's job is stopping pucks. You see where most players are on the ice and can warn your teammates when you anticipate danger. This will help them clear your zone or check a man and prevent goals. If you control the puck and no one calls for it, shoot it to a corner of the rink. Do not take a chance in passing it to a teammate standing in front of the net.

Never criticize your teammates, You need their cooperation, so talk to help them, not to criticize; leave that to the coach. Your job is to correct all the mistakes you can.

To prevent these mistakes, follow the system established by your coach. The sooner you work it out, the better you will play.

HOW TO PREPARE YOURSELF MENTALLY FOR A GAME

Since you face many players and shots during every game, review in advance the players you will face. Note their strong points and tell your teammates so they will be better prepared to help you defend the goal.

Some players shoot hard; some always shoot high or low; some shoot for the far side or the short side; deke on their back-hand or their forehand; pass the puck after a false shot; shoot from the wrong foot; try to shoot when a player screens you. If you think about this only when you step on the ice for the game, you won't be ready. Prepare yourself the night before or the day of the game!

HOW TO WATCH PLAYER CHANGES DURING PLAY

Not enough attention is paid to the player changes during play. Forwards can get away with this mistake, but a goalie cannot forget, since he is the last line of defense on his team. If the goalie doesn't notice when a player with a weak shot is replaced by a Bobby Hull, the puck will be in the net before he realizes what happened. You should watch the superstars very closely, because they can catch you off balance with one move of the wrist. Know who is on the ice at all times.

Know your own players, too. Some of them like to gamble with the puck or do not stick to their positions. If you are aware of their individual peculiarities, you can adjust your style accordingly. As I said earlier, you are there to correct all the mistakes you can, so be alert.

HOW TO OVERCOME FEAR OF THE PUCK

When a goalie is afraid of being hit by the puck, he tends to lift his shoulders up and back. If you sometimes lift up when a player slaps the puck, bring your shoulders in, move toward him very slowly and keep your chest tilted forward. This will help you to leave your stick on the ice and should correct your problem.

Sometimes a goalie will tend to lift on slap shots, a move that can be very costly, especially on the low ones. To find out if you have this fault, notice if you jump to make chest saves against high shots from about thirty feet. On those shots, you should crouch to stop the puck and duck the high ones, not stand up and lift.

When you lift, you move with the wind-up rather than the puck. Therefore you are off balance for the shots along the ice, which then give you trouble, even on very bad angles.

Goalies also tend to lift when a teammate puts his stick in front of a shot to try to stop it. To overcome this fear, crouch a little more- not too much, so you'll still be ready for a high shot. Then if the puck misses the stick, you'll be in position to stop it.

You might fear a slap shot after an injury above the waist or when a player who once hurt you on a high shot is winding up again from the same place. If you lift, bring in your shoulders and move slowly forward. It will help, but you might be slow to move for a while because you tighten up too much as the player slaps the puck.

Inadequate equipment may also be to blame for this problem. When a goalie is not protected enough, he gets hurt every time out and fears the hard shots as a result. In many cases, good equipment can solve the problem.

Fear is human. We all experience it at one time or another. But, if you always fear injuries, give up goaltending. You are not cut out to be a goalie.

5 WHAT TO DO ON GAME DAY

First, stay off your feet the day of a game. Since the goalie remains on his feet throughout the game, most of the time in a crouch, walking adds to the strain he puts on his legs. When they tire, he moves more slowly, falls down more, stays down longer, doesn't crouch as much to follow the screen shots, doesn't think as fast, and thus loses his concentration.

Concentration is most important. The goalie must be alert and on his toes, ready to jump on a loose puck or follow it wherever it goes. He can foresee danger help his teammates prevent it.

Even reading can affect your game, because it tires eyes as well as your mind. Read for a couple of minutes and then notice how you feel when you get up. Why do you think many people read themselves to sleep?

If you can get some sleep on the afternoon of a game you'll notice a change in your performance. Sleep rests your and your mind. One or two hours is enough to relax you and sharpen your reflexes.

Another important element of the day is your food. Most young players eat with their families an hour or so before the game. The food is sometimes too heavy for a hockey player — it's hard to digest and makes you feel slow and lazy. It can also repeat on you. Salty food is bad because it makes you thirsty, and drinking should be avoided during play. If you cannot change your meals, at least don't eat a great deal, and don't eat heavy desserts.

Go to bed early the night before a game to relax a ready the next day. You will see the puck as big as a football and move as fast as a cat to pick it up.

These small details, added to your knowledge of the game, will help you play better and can make the difference between just a goalie, a good goalie, a star, and a superstar. Which one do you want to be?

6 "V" OR "BUTTERFLY" STYLE

This book wouldn't be complete without mention of the "V" or "butterfly" style. This style of playing goal was invented by Glenn Hall in the early 1950's. When he began using it, most experts said that he'd never succeed playing goal that way. But Glenn bad a brilliant career in the NHL and proved once again that the style of goal-tending is not the be all and end all of a career. Only the results are kept in the record book.

Many goalies tried to copy Glenn, but very few succeeded, either because their reflexes weren't fast enough or they didn't know how to use this style to their advantage. I played with Glenn for two years, in St. Louis, and watched him very closely. I tried that style for a while, only to have Glenn advise me against using it generally. Now I only use it in a few, special situations.

As I mentioned elsewhere in this book, I have been reading, listening, and watching for more than thirty years in order to improve my game. That is how I found out that the "V" style is useful on certain screen shots, deflections, and shots that will miss the net if the puck doesn't hit something along the way. In this last case, I often use the "V" style . Many times, to my surprise the puck was deflected and hit me, when it would have been a goal had I stayed up, expecting it to miss the net.

The above is all I personally know about the "V" style. The tips that follow come from the one of the best goalies ever in professional hockey: Tony Esposito. I watched him continually after he went to the Black Hawks and couldn't understand how he could move so quickly to his knees and get up in time to cover up on a rebound or a loose puck.

I talked to Tony about this book, and when I asked him for help, he immediately agreed to answer my questions. I am most grateful for his cooperation and I hope you will benefit from his knowledge.

Jacques: With the curved sticks and the slap shots, do you think young goalies should use the "V" style, stand up, or use both styles?

Tony: Either, whichever is more comfortable for the individual.

Jacques: If a young goalie uses the "V" style, will he be able to play that way all his life or have to change as he gets older?

The "V" style: stance at the edge of the crease

Tony: He can use this style as long as he stays in excellent condition. If he doesn't, it would be very difficult.

Jacques: Where do you stand when you follow the play from the other end of the rink?

Tony: Nowhere in particular. I just try to keep moving around to keep my reflexes sharp.

Jacques: When do you move out?

Tony: When the opposition is coming out of their end, I will move outside the crease (about five feet).

The "V" style : following the puck on screen shots

Jacques: When do you move back?

Tony: I will move back when the opposition crosses our blue line.

Jacques: How far back do you move?

Tony: I move back to approximately the edge of the crease. This is where I would like to make the save.

Jacques: How do you find your net without looking back?

Tony: I use the face-off circles. I'll glance back once in a while if I have time. Also through constant practice.

Jacques: When the puck is inside your zone, how do you move with it? Do you stay outside your goal crease or back against the goal line?

Tony: I try to stay on the edge of the crease.

The "V" style: Going down for the save

Jacques: How do you look for the screen shots from the blue line?

Tony: I get down low and look through the legs of the players. If I can't see the puck, I'll go down on my knees and try to cover as much net as possible.

Jacques: Do you stand up to play the shots from the blue line or go down with the shot?

Tony: If the shot is low, usually I'll go down.

Jacques: On a breakaway down center ice, where do you wait for the puck carrier?

Tony: At about five to seven feet outside the crease.

Jacques: Do you play the player to shoot or to deke you on a breakaway?

Tony: I try to force the player to deke by backing in slowly and not giving him much net.

Jacques: On a shot from close in, do you stand up or go down?

Tony: Most of the time I go down.

Jacques: If you go down, when do you? After the shot is taken or as the player winds up?

Tony: After the shot is taken, unless the player is very close to me. I try not to anticipate, but sometimes I do by mistake.

Jacques: What do you have to watch most because of your style? Going down too soon?

Tony: This is very important. I don't go down until the shot is taken unless the shooter is very close to me.

Jacques: How about staying down too long?

Tony: As soon as I make a save I get up quickly. This is the key to playing my style.

Jacques: How do you handle high shots from close in?

Tony: I try to move out a little, then go to my knees. As a result, the shooter has very little net.

Jacques: Are you more vulnerable on high shots from close in than the stand-up goalies?

Tony: I am more vulnerable to high shots from close in just as a standing goalie is vulnerable to low shots. I feel it's harder to pick the top corners than the lower ones.

Jacques: Can a goalie combine the two styles and play well?

Tony: Perhaps. Against certain teams I'll stand up more than others. A goalie can use a combination of the styles but not completely change from one to the other.

Jacques: Why don't you wrap your foot around the goal post, as Glenn Hall did, when the puck is behind the goal line?

Tony: Because that makes it more difficult to move across the net when the puck is shot out front.

Jacques: On a two-on-one breakaway, how do you want your defenseman to play?

Tony: I like the defenseman to force the puck carrier wide, then as he gets close to the net, move on him and force him to either shoot quickly or pass the puck. This makes the puck carrier *rush*, so he'll be more likely to make mistakes. If the defenseman stays in the middle and lets the man shoot at his own leisure, he'll have a good chance to score.

If the shooter is rushed, he must make a quick decision: Shoot or pass. If he shoots it will be in a hurry. If he passes, the other man will have to pick up the pass and get the shot off. If the puck is passed, I dive or slide to get over to the other player and hope the puck hits me or else misses the net.

Jacques: What lie stick do you suggest for goalies using your style?

Tony: It depends on his height. A goalie about 5'11" should use a lie 13. If he is shorter, 11 or 12. If he is taller, 14 or 15.

Jacques: On a corner face-off, where do you advise the goalie to position himself?

Tony: If the opposing center is good on draws, I move a little to face the man in position to take the shot. Otherwise I face the circle.

Tony Esposito playing for Team Canada in the 1972 Canada-U.S.S.R. series

Jacques: Where do you get hurt most, and what did you do to protect yourself?

Tony: The arms. I have added sponge to my arm pads.

Jacques: On an angle shot how do you stand? a) When the shooter is near the boards?

Tony: I stand up holding the post.

b) When the shooter is 20 feet away?

Tony: In my normal crouch position, with my legs apart.

c) When the shooter comes closer?

Tony: In my normal crouch position with my legs apart.

Then after answering my questions, Tony added the following tips: The keys to the "Butterfly," or what I call the "V" style:

1. Be in top physical condition: *You must be able to get up quickly after the save.*

2. Try not to commit yourself until the shot is taken.

3. Play the angles. When you go down, you have to move out to the edge of the crease or you'll give the shooter too much net.

Advantages of the "V" Style.

1. Fewer rebounds because you play more pucks with the body rather than the pads.

2. Fewer goals along the ice.

3. Fewer goals on screen shots because you are low and most screen shots are low.

Disadvantages of the "V" Style

1. High corners are left open.

2. More goals may come in between the legs.

After reading Tony's answers, you can see that, even though he uses a different style, the basic moves and positions are all the same as those the stand-up goalie uses.

He plays the shots from the edge of the crease, stands up after every save, follows the puck between the legs of the players on screen shots from the blue line, waits for the shot before moving, and doesn't anticipate plays.

He stresses *top physical condition.*

I also asked Tony Esposito if his wearing contact lenses affects his game.

He replied that if it does, he's never noticed it and hopes that no young goalie will give up goaltending because he needs glasses. This problem can be corrected as soon as he is old enough to wear contact lenses.

Vladislav Tretiak, goalie for the U.S.S.R. National Team in action against Team Canada

7 HOW TO COACH

YOUNG GOALIES

The goalie is the most important player on your team; he must not have a bad game, and his training should come first, With the proper practices, he will improve faster, have fewer bad games, and make your work much easier.

Don't worry about the size of your goalie. Players like Charlie Hodges, Gump Worsley, Gilles Villemure, and Rogatien Vachon all made it to the N.H..L at about 5'8".

Make sure your goalie is not a quitter, but a fighter. He should get angry at himself after every goal, rather than feel sorry for himself.

Teach your goalie to report every injury he suffers. If you decide to play him despite his injuries, do not expect him to perform at his best, and don't accuse him of not trying if he plays badly, This treatment could affect him for the rest of his hockey career.

Now let's see what we can do to help the young ones improve their game, slowly but surely.

SKATING

Skating is the most important part of the goalie's game. How can he stop the puck, clear a rebound, or control the puck if he cannot skate or loses his balance after each save?

Here are a few skating exercises to help a beginner.

1. Put one skate behind the other to form a "T". Push once with the back foot and stop immediately on the back skate right away, keeping the "T" position. Repeat the exercise, moving across the ice. Change feet to come back.

This exercise will help him achieve maximum power with each stride and improve his balance.

2. From the "T" position, take three strides, glide about five feet on one skate and stop on the back foot, keeping the "T" position. Skate the length of the ice and come back using the other leg.

3. From the "T" position, take three strides and stop on both skates, facing to the right. Repeat the exercise down the length of the ice. Come back facing to the left.

4. Same exercise as 3, but stop on the inside foot. Change feet coming back.

5. Same exercise as 3, but stop on the outside foot. Change feet coming back.

6. Same exercise as 3, but stop on the inside skate and pivot in one motion, to go forward without losing a second. Do this exercise between the blue lines and the red line. Pivot to the right in one direction and to the left in the other.

Skating Exercise 3

7. Same exercise as 3, but stop on the front foot and skate backward. Do this exercise between the blue lines and the red line, changing feet each time.

8. Skate around the face-off circles, crossing the leg over as you turn instead of pushing with the back skate. Practise turning in both directions.

9. Same exercise as 8 but skate backward, pushing with the inside foot and crossing it behind the other leg. To achieve this, you must bring the leg out and pull back to give more power and speed. Turn in both directions.

CONDITIONING

Young boys are so loose that they do not need as much training as the older ones. But they should exercise the hamstring and groin muscles, as well as the arms, hands, wrists, and ankles for more strength. See Chapter 2 for the exercises. Naturally, ping-pong is very much recommended, as it speeds up the reflexes.

EQUIPMENT

Make sure your goalie is well protected from the beginning, so he will not give up playing goal because of injuries due to bad equipment. When the young ones start, their parents very seldom buy them much in the way of equipment, because they do not know how serious the boy is about hockey or because they cannot afford to. So the goalie has to use what is available. Take a look at his equipment and ask yourself if you would play with it. If not, do something about it. If all coaches complain when they should, the equipment will have to improve. Unfortunately, too few people know enough about goaltenders to really care about their equipment. But now you do, so please help them so they can help you.

See the notes on equipment in Chapter 3 and in the Appendix.

THE PROPER STANCE

A goalie can have all the equipment he needs, but if he doesn't stand properly, he'll never be a good goalie. He will be inclined to fall down too soon or too often, allow easy shots along the ice, have trouble making stick saves, and give a lot of rebounds.

First he must use goalie skates for better balance. Regular skates do not have enough blade in contact with the ice and consequently force the goalie to stand on his toes or his heels. The weight should be on the balls of the feet, with the knees slightly bent (as for playing ping-pong) and the legs apart the width of the shoulders. If the goalie uses the right stick (that is, if the thick part is the right length), his back-hand glove should touch the outside top of his pad. The opening of the catching glove should always face the puck and rest knee-high and even with the pad, not in front of it.

Make sure the top of the body is slightly tilted forward. When the goalie stands too straight, his weight shifts to his heels and his knees are either bent too much or almost straight, resulting in soft goals on shots about one foot off the ice.

HOW TO SLIDE ACROSS THE GOAL LINE

Most of the time, the young goalies cannot move from one side of the net to the other in one push, but as long as they keep the front skate sideways, they can push as often as they have to.

Pushing sideways is very important because it helps the goalie to play better in so many ways. First, it reminds him to put his skate, not his pad, against the goal post. Second, it helps him to stand up and face the front of the net, ready for a save. Third, it gives him a chance to put his stick outside the goal post to prevent a pass coming in from behind the goal. Fourth, it makes him practice keeping his skate against the goal post every time the puck goes behind the goal line so he is ready for a possible pass to the front of the net. And finally, it enables him to follow the puck out of the corner of his eye, rather than turn his body, when a player carries the puck behind the net.

THE STICK

Make sure the goalie holds his stick at the shoulders with one finger on top for a stronger grip. He should always hold it this way- to make a save, to stop the puck behind the net, to clear the puck on his back-hand, and to prevent a pass from behind the goal line. The only time the goalie moves his hand up is to poke the puck away from a player or to use both hands.

SHOOTING EXERCISE

Line the players up at the blue line and make them shoot, not slap, the puck from about thirty feet out to exercise your goalie.

Make him:

catch the puck,

use his back-hand glove,

use his skate only on the stick side,

use his pads to stop the shots (but not kick the puck),

stand up at the edge of the goal crease to face the puck, not go back as the players move in,

keep his feet still while waiting for the shot (not move the knees and skates like a marionette),

drop the puck after catching it and pass it to the side with the back-hand (holding the stick at the shoulders with one hand),

drop the puck after catching it and pass it up front to the next shooter at the blue line (using two hands on his stick),

stand up, not dropping a knee to the ice, to make a save, (when the puck comes hard enough) steer it- to the corner in one motion.

During this shooting exercise, make your goalie stand up with legs apart the width of the shoulders, the catching glove open, resting knee-high and even, not in front of the pads, and grip his stick with one finger on the shoulders rather than hold it by the handle.

The goalie can move forward very slowly to stop the puck but never backward. If he does, his weight will shift to the heels, his stick will come off the ice, and he will be off balance, forcing him to go down on the ice to make a save. (This is good only with the butterfly style). I would suggest you teach him to stand up first and let him decide later on the style he prefers to use.

Anticipating a deflection by No. 17 of the St. Louis Blues

If your goalie lifts up on almost every slap shot and fears injuries, even if he has not been hurt, point out this fault to him and make him bring in his shoulders to overcome the habit. If he continues to do so all the time, he does not belong in the net.

This shooting exercise will help your goalie only if the players stay out at the proper distance and do not slap the puck.

They should sometimes lift the puck and other times shoot along the ice, forcing the goalie to play each shot as it comes. He should not be allowed to get set, like a robot, to play the low shots, then hold his stick off the ice knowing the high shots are coming.

The low shots will make him practice deflecting the puck, stopping it, and passing it with two hands, using his skate on the back-

Keeping my eye on the puck as Bobby Orr circles the net

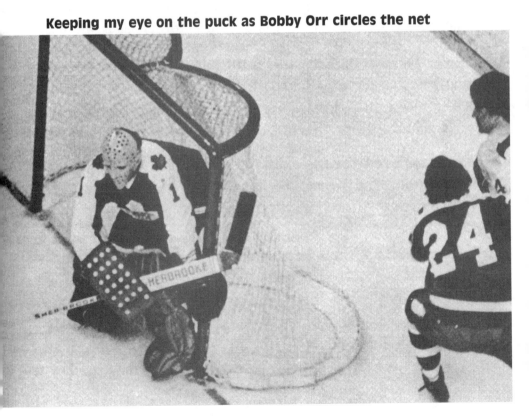

hand side or the stick if it is close to him. The high ones will test his catching and back-hand gloves. He will have to catch the puck and pass it with one or two hands on his stick. He will learn to kill the rebounds, not kick the puck in front with his pads. He will practice standing up for a save, not dropping one knee to the ice. The shots from the slot help your goalie to stand at the edge of his goal crease and face the puck, rather than backing away.

Passing the puck is quite difficult for a goalie, and practicing it with a teammate is boring. This way it is easier. To add some interest in his exercise, tell the players they have to score so many goals each time. This will make them try harder and keep your goalie on his toes.

When the goalie works hard on this kind of practise, he tends to go down, thinking he will stop more shots this way. He often favours his catching glove, and gives a lot of rebounds with his pads and stick. Make him hold his stance at the edge of the goal crease. If he handles himself well during these contests, he will do the same during the games and enjoy playing more. It is up to the coach to make the practices interesting as he teaches the players how to play the game.

To find out how good you are at this, listen to the team after practice. If they say, "The practice went by fast," you're succeeding.

HOW TO COVER THE ANGLES

A goaltender should always be aware of the location of the puck on the ice and cover his angles accordingly. He should be alert at all times, especially when the puck is about thirty feet from the net and at a bad angle. A lot of goals are scored from there because the goalie turns his body toward the front of the net as he puts his foot against the goal post, instead of facing the puck.

Sometimes the goalie expecting a pass across the net will lean forward to play it and let in a goal on the short side, at the top.

Many rebounds are also scored from just in front of the goal line because the goalies are not ready for those shots. If they would realize that a puck in front of the goal line can go into the net, they would regain their defensive position faster and control most of those shots.

The same principle applies when a player dekes a defenseman to end up just in front of the goal line. The goalie should always play him to shoot, not anticipate a pass. The only time he plays the pass is when the puck is behind the goal line.

A good exercise to make goalies practice their angles and position themselves with the puck is to send the players along the boards and make them shoot from around the face-off circle (no slap shots). The coach can stand there to force the players to move around him. Send the players from both sides of the ice, and let them also use their back-hand shots. This will help the goalie to face the puck instead of lifting and backing away.

When the goalies are very young, don't let the players cross in front of the net with the puck. Young goalies wear too much equipment to stand up and cannot move quickly after the puck unless they dive for it, a habit which will have to be corrected as they mature.

HOW TO FOLLOW THE PUCK

Since it is the goalie's job to stop the puck, he should learn right from the start how to keep track of its whereabouts at all times, even with a lot of players in front of him.

Teach him to look between the players' legs, not over their shoulders on shots from the point. At the same time, remind your goalie to hold his stick at the shoulders and keep it close to the ice, to make a save with the thick part.

If he makes a save with the thick part of his stick and wants to freeze the puck with his glove, make him put his stick in front of it, not behind, so no one will poke the puck away from him.

Tell your goalie to use his glove or stick to pass the puck to a teammate standing away from the net and to the side not in front, whenever he has time.

HOW TO PLAY SCREEN SHOTS FROM CLOSE IN

Most young goalies have a lot of trouble playing the puck when they are screened, because they don't try hard enough to see the puck, or when they do, they feel they must hit the ice to make a save.

To correct this problem practice some one-on-one, making the puck-carrier shoot as he gets close to the defense. The goalie will learn to look from the right side, keep his balance, and stand up. Make sure he holds his ground in a semi-crouch position, rather than move backward into the net. I say "semi-crouch" because he has to lean to the side of the puck to see it and at the same time be ready to move fast if the puck goes to the far side.

HOW TO STOP THE PUCK BEH1ND THE GOAL

I haven't mentioned this earlier because the younger players don't shoot the puck hard enough to send it around the boards, from outside the blue line; the blue line is the guide line-on shots from the blue line the goalie can go out and come back in plenty of time. Only the best goalies can take chances on shots from inside the blue line, but they must move very fast, because in this situation there is always an opponent ready to check them.

In the equipment chapter I mentioned the importance of goalie skates; without them a goalie cannot play well. His balance is never right. He has to work very hard to stand up, loses a split second to move after the puck, and, if he stops it, often has to drop one knee to hold his balance. A goalie can have all the ability in the world and the best equipment, but without goalie skates he will always have some problems on certain shots. It's like an outfielder in baseball playing on grass wearing running shoes, He'll catch the fly balls hit at him, but if he has to break fast or stop fast to catch one, he'll often slide and miss it. If your goalie is in this situation don't criticize him, but encourage him by saying that it will all improve when he plays with goalie skates.

These notes on coaching beginners are simply a guide to help you. If your goalie is a step ahead of his class, teach him the more advanced lessons that follow. But don't go too fast, or he might find it too bard, start fighting the puck, and lose his timing. Too much instruction can mix him up and hinder rather than help him.

Exercising during Training Camp, 1972

8 HOW TO COACH ADVANCED GOALIES

Too many coaches put too much pressure on their goalies and forget that their state of mind is as important as their physical condition. There is nothing worse for goalies than constant criticism. All goalies think alike and all fear playing badly; consequently, they all feel the same pressure every time they are scheduled to play a game. They know that the slightest mistake can cost them a goal; they'll become touchy and sometimes a little difficult to deal with.

Meet regularly with them to detect any change in their attitude and try to prevent a letdown. Communications between the goalies and their coach is of utmost importance. They must feel that he cares about them if they are to give their best.

Goalies are also affected by their equipment, playing conditions, and the kind of practices and training methods used by their coach. No matter how talented they are, if they aren't happy, they won't perform as well as they should. Draw up a master plan for your goalies, with a progression of minor aims for them to achieve. This will bring out the best in them.

Working goalies hard does not guarantee that they will improve. But moderate exercises will correct their weaknesses. When the exercises are too difficult, your goalies will tire quickly and cannot take full advantage of them.

Since goalies are more likely to pull their groin and hamstring muscles than other players are, they should exercise every day at home or before putting on their equipment. It takes only five minutes and is well worth it. (See Chapter 2.)

Goalies are worth between 50 to 65 per cent of their team, and for that reason, the coaches should spend a little more time with them. Make the defensemen adjust their style to your goalie's, not the other way around, or you'll encounter a lot of problems. And finally, run your practices according to your goalie's capacities and talent, not according to what other coaches do. Here is the kind of practice I use-to improve my concentration, maintain my reflexes, and coordinate my game with my defensemen:

SKATING EXERCISES

1. Before each practice, hold a light skating drill to warm everybody up. When drills are too tough, the players won't perform well during the rest of the practice. If you think the players need more conditioning, save the hard drills for the end.

2. Make every player (except the goalies) skate behind the net during warm-up drills to keep the ice in good condition for shooting exercises and line rushes.

WARM-UP EXERCISES

1. Have about five minutes of shots on the goalies before the start of each practice, but after the skating drills.

2. Line up the players at the blue line and make them shoot from the slot. Don't allow high shots, slap shots, or deking; you are warming up the goalies, not trying to score goals.

3. Don't make the players carry the puck from one end of the rink to the other before they shoot at the net. This is the worst way I know for a goalie to warm up, because at the beginning of a practice, he is tight and fears being hurt. Watch your goalies lift up when certain players wind up to slap the puck, and you'll see what I mean.

Players who deke the goalie in warm-up exercises also risk making him pull a muscle. I recommend they stick to wrist shots from the slot or slap shots from the point (blue line).

After the shots, the goalies are ready for the line rushes ... with *low* slap shots and players who will try to deke. Notice that I said *low* slap shots. Goalies are not targets to be shot at, and the mask does not mean that every shot is permitted. If you want your goalies to improve (and I'm sure you do), don't let the players shoot high at them. This should help them play better during the league games, because they will not fear the high shots so much.

LINE RUSHES

During line rushes everybody works: The offence tries to score, the defense and goalie cooperate to stop them.

The first thing you must do is establish a system between your defensemen and your goalies, so they learn to talk to and understand one another—a must if they are to perform well.

Change defensemen after each rush to give them a rest and help them practice better.

Blow the whistle each time a player gambles or moves out of position in anticipating a play. This kind of reminder will help them to avoid the same mistake in regular games. A defenseman cannot gamble with the puck, because most of the time he is the last man between his opponent and the goal. When he does, the goalie should caution him not to try it again, and the coach should warn him in a more direct way.

Don't blow the whistle too soon on line rushes, so that the players can maintain their aggressiveness in chasing the puck. This aggressiveness must be drilled into them, and is achieved only through practices. Let the play go, but make the players hold their positions rather than skate all over the ice after the puck.

So far, I have said very little about the goalie. It is impossible to teach goaltending and forget the defensemen, because each needs the other to neutralize every offensive formation. The goalie is part of a team that must work as a unit. When everyone plays his position, the goalie can perform better and his team is usually a winner.

You can't tell how good a goalie is until he plays behind a defense. He may look very good on solo shots and be 'way off when players start passing the puck around. That's why I say that there's more to goaltending than just stopping pucks. A goalie must continually study himself and adjust with the teams and the formations he plays against.

This is how the defensemen must play to help their goalie:

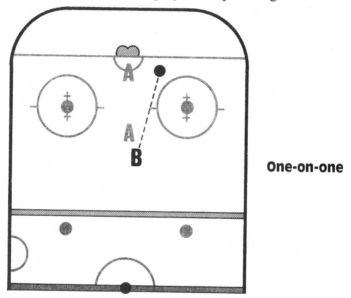

One-on-one

ONE-ON-ONE

On one-on-one rushes, the defenseman should say to himself, "I don't want to touch the puck." He should just follow the puck carrier to one side or the other (not lunge forward to poke the puck away from him or try to hit him), and make him shoot from an angle. This helps the goalie to cover his angles and clear the rebound if he can.

When the puck carrier slides the puck past the defenseman in front of the net, the goalie skates out to control the puck while the defenseman plays the opponent. The goalie must play the puck in case his defenseman misses his check, who could then pick it up and shoot on the net.

Results

One-on-one helps the *puck carrier* to deke the defenseman or to beat the goalie with a quick screen shot. It forces the *defenseman* to *follow* the puck carrier rather than lunge at the puck or try to hit him, and reminds him to stay with his check after the shot to give the goalie time to clear the rebound or control the puck. One-on-one makes the *goalie* practice:

his angles,

screen shots from close in,

skating out of the net and controlling the loose pucks,

handling the puck with his stick,

deflecting the puck with his stick,

controlling the rebounds.

TWO-ON-ONE

In two-on-one, the defenseman stays even with the net to force the puck carrier to shoot from an angle, watches for the pass to the open man, and goes for the rebound as soon as the puck is shot.

The defenseman does not try to take the puck away from his opponent or try to hit him, because if he misses, the two players can be all alone with the goalie.

The defenseman watches for the pass and lets his goalie play the shot, but he must play the rebound as soon as the puck is shot.

If the puck carrier tries to cut in front of the net, the defenseman must play him and hope the pass to the open man will not be completed.

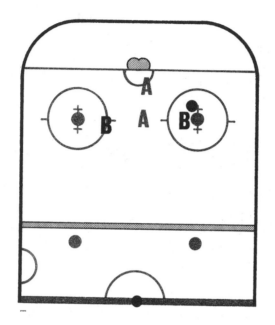

Two-on-one

Results

Two-on-one helps the *defenseman* to hold his position in line with the net, reminds him to prevent his opponent from cutting in on the goalie, reminds him how to play rebounds and to clear not carry them away from the front of the net.

In two-on-one the *attackers* practice beating the defenseman and moving toward the net for a deflection, a pass, or a rebound; they learn to pass the puck by the defenseman or to interfere with him after a drop pass.

The *goalie* practices:

his angles,

holding his ground and facing the shooter when he comes in, instead of backing into the net or dropping one knee to the ice to make a save, moving across the goal crease if a pass is attempted to the open man,

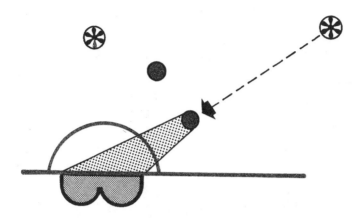

Forcing the puck carrier to shoot from an angle

adjusting in a hurry when his defensemen let the puck carrier cross in front of the net, poking the puck away from the player trying to deke him,

playing screen shots from close in if the puck is shot from the middle,

clearing rebounds or freezing the puck, because of the open man standing in front of the net, playing deflections.

THREE-ON-ONE

On three-on-one, with the puck carrier along the boards, the defenseman stays in line with the net, as in two-on-one and watches for the pass to the far man.

If the pass goes to the slot man, the defenseman does not move forward for the puck, because if he misses the puck can go to one of the two players skating in from both sides of the net.

After a shot is taken at the net, the defenseman plays the rebound and shoots it—rather than carries it—to the corner, if the puck is

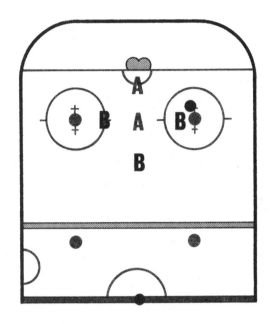

Three-on-one

in front of the net.

The goalie does not move to block his angles as he does in one-on-one or two-on-one, because the puck carrier has two players to pass the puck to. If the goalie is too far out, he will not recover in time to stop the puck if it goes to the far man.

Results

The *defenseman* learns to skate even with the net, to watch the pass to the man skating on the far side, to stand up rather than try to block shots, to prevent the puck carrier from cutting in front of the net, to clear the rebounds—not carry the puck—away from the net.

The *offense* learns to beat the defenseman, to deflect the puck, to return a pass to an open man if the goalie can make a save on them, to jump on the rebounds instead of skating away from the net.

The *goalie* practices:

his angles,

moving across his goal crease in a hurry if a pass is attempted to the far man coming in behind him, clearing the rebounds or freezing the puck, because of the two opponents standing near his goal, playing screen shots from close in, if the puck is shot from the middle,

playing deflections.

TWO-ON-TWO

The defensemen play two-on-two like one-on-one, one following the puck carrier and forcing him to shoot from an angle while the other defenseman watches for the pass to the open man, and the rebound.

The goalie blocks his angles as in one-on-one and plays the puck in front of the net when the player slides it past his defenseman.

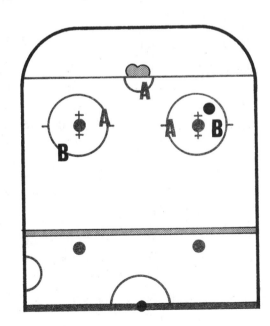

Two-on-two

Results

The *defensemen* learn to hold their positions and back each other up. They also remember not to lunge after the puck carrier to try to hit him, but to follow him and force him to shoot from an angle; they practice checking the open forward and going after the rebounds.

The *offense* practice beating around the defense, moving into position to receive a pass, and skating toward the net for a deflection or a rebound.

The *goalie* practices:

his angles,

puck handling when he chases loose pucks and rebounds,

stopping screen shots from close in, if the play comes from the middle,

freezing the puck when the open man moves in for the rebound,

playing deflections.

THREE-ON-TWO

Most mistakes are made when three forwards attack, but if the defensemen play their positions, they can usually neutralize them quite easily.

When the play comes from the side, one defenseman plays the puck carrier as in one-on-one, while the other one watches for the pass to the far man.

When the play comes from the middle, the two defensemen hold their positions and let their goalie play the shot. But if a pass goes to a wingman, the defenseman on that side forces him to shoot from an angle, while his teammate watches for the pass to the far man standing behind the goalie.

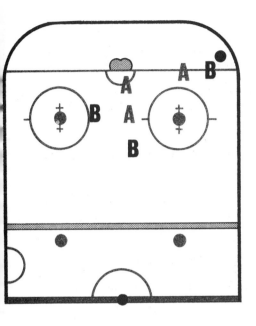

Three-on-two

I cannot understand why most defensemen almost always watch the slot man first, even after they have been told not to. The goalie has a chance to stop the slot man, but none against the player standing behind him.

The defensemen need a lot of practice to coordinate their moves against three-on-two, because they can easily be drawn out of position when the puck goes from one side of the net to the other—behind the goal line, in front of the goal line, to the point, to the slot man, back in the corner, and so forth.

It sounds complicated, doesn't it? How would you like to be the goalie trying to adjust with each puck movement when your defensemen get all mixed up? Here is the only way to defend against three-on-two:

When the Puck is behind the Goal Line

One defenseman plays the puck carrier and the other one stays about a stick's length in front of the goal crease, not at the edge of it, and watches the pass to the slot man. The goalie checks the pass to the forward standing behind him. The defenseman playing the puck carrier cannot let him come back in front of the goal line with the puck, or his team will be in trouble.

When the Puck is in front of the Goal Line

When the puck is in front of the goal line, it can be shot into the net; the goalie must play it and not anticipate a pass to the player standing behind him. That player belongs to the open defenseman, who must check him first, not the slot man. The defenseman rushes the slot man only when the puck is passed to him.

If the defensemen remember this and swivel with the puck, they will neutralize the best attacks.

Results

Three-on-two is the best exercise for the *defensemen*. Because the slightest mistake can cost them a goal, they must think "positional hockey" all the time, and make sure the puck carrier doesn't deke them.

They practice clearing rebounds, forcing the puck carrier to shoot from an angle, and watching for a pass to an open man, behind or in front of the net. Their coordination here is very important, because the goalie is at their mercy.

The *offense* learns to stay away from one another to open up the defense, to pass the puck and not try to deke the defense. They learn to be more aggressive; to position themselves to receive a pass; to regain the puck from the defense, to keep a man in a scoring position in the slot or behind the goalie (rather than having all three players behind the goal line, chasing the puck); to keep their sticks on the ice, ready to shoot on the net or to pass the puck back to an open man when they see no chance to score from their position.

The *goalie* practices:

his angles,

moving to the middle of his goal crease when the puck goes to the slot man,

regaining his net if the slot man passes the puck to one side of the net instead of shooting,

playing screen shots from close in when the puck comes from the middle,

intercepting corner passes or passes from behind the net, while holding his stick at the shoulders,

facing the front of the net when the puck is behind the net,

not anticipating a pass,

poking the puck away from a player trying to cut in front of the net,

moving from one post to the other with the blade of his stick preceding him, when the puck is carried across the back of the net by an opponent,

deflecting rebounds away from the front of his net,

freezing the puck, because of all the players moving around him,

standing up, to be ready for a rebound, a quick pass, a deke, or to go after a loose puck,

facing the shooter, not backing away from him or dropping a knee to the ice to make a save,

playing deflections.

FIVE-ON-TWO

Although five-on-two doesn't occur in a game, it helps to remind the forwards to pass the puck early to the point man, instead of at the last moment or in a desperate move.

In five-on-two, the defensemen must play their positions to perfection and cooperate fully with their goalie, because the puck can go from the point, to either of the men standing beside the net, to the slot man; the point man can also pass the puck across the ice for as many plays from that side. If the defensemen run all over the ice, they will find themselves out of position in no time, with the puck in their net.

During this exercise, do not allow the point men to shoot the puck past the edge of the face-off circles, because the defensemen must stay back, as in a game, and not rush the shooter.

After the players hold their positions, send in a forward to help the defense and make it five-on-three. This forward will force the offense to be more careful when passing the puck and more aggressive in controlling it or regaining it from the defensive team.

Finally, send in two forwards and practice the power play. Starting with five-on-two helps the defensemen to understand each other and cooperate with the goalie. The forwards sent in increase the defense's coordination; the defensemen will learn that if they hold their positions, depending on who comes back to help them, they will handle most offensive formations.

Results

The *defensemen* play as in three-on-two; they also learn to clear the way so their goalie can see the puck on shots from the points. They move to the outside of the net, not to the middle, and check the open man standing beside the net, waiting to deflect the puck or jump on the rebound. They practice clearing the puck, not carrying it, away from the front of the net.

The *offense* passes the puck as in three-on-two; they also learn to use the point men. They practise deflecting the puck from the point, stopping it for a quick shot at the net, a deke, or a pass to an open man, if the goalie is in a position to stop them; they learn to go after the rebounds.

The *goalie* plays as in three-on-two, and also practices:

playing screen shots from the blue line,

stopping the deflections on shots from the blue line,

following the puck between the players' legs, not over their shoulders, while holding the thick part of his stick near the ice,

catching the puck from a crouch position, to hold it, deflect it, or freeze it, depending on the players surrounding him.

Line rushes are important to everybody on your team. The offense learns puck control, to play positional hockey and be ready to receive a pass, and aggressiveness; the defense—positional hockey and cooperation with their goalie; the goalie—how to adjust continually with each offensive formation and movement of the puck.

Be very careful with these exercises. They can help your team, but they can also hurt it if the players skate all over the ice and don't hold their positions. Blow the whistle every time they wander, and impress upon them the risks they are taking. The sooner they learn to stick to their positions, the better they will play.

EXERCISE WITH A DEFENSEMAN
CHASING THE PUCK CARRIER

While line rushes are good, other exercises will help your goalie to react faster and adjust with the puck carrier.

A good one is to line the players up against the boards at the far blue line and make them skate down the ice. (Keep the defensemen at center ice with you.) Pass the puck to the forwards as they reach the red line and send a defenseman after them at the same time. Sometimes the defense will force the forwards to shoot from an angle; if the defenseman can't catch up with the forwards, they will have a chance to cut in front of the net.

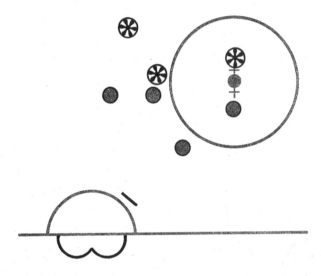

Opposing players to watch on corner face-off

Results

The *defensemen* learn to chase the puck carrier and force him to shoot from an angle, and to go for rebounds.

This exercise will help the *offense* to pick up speed as they approach the net, instead of slowing down as most do. It will help them to decide to shoot or when to cut in front of the net. They will also practice going for the net in case of a rebound. The forwards playing the wrong wing will practice their back-band and may even find new ways to beat the goalies.

On these rushes, the *goalie* practices:

his angles,

poking the puck away from the player cutting in front of the net,

moving in a crouch position toward the puck carrier when he cuts away from the net, transferring his weight from one leg to the other and pushing with the back skate while holding his stick at the shoulders.

EXERCISE WITH PLAYERS CUTTING TWENTY FEET AWAY FROM THE GOALIE

Line the players up at the blue line and make them cut in about twenty feet in front of the net, forcing the goalie to move with them and toward them, not along the edge of the goal crease or backward into the net.

Don't let the players shoot for the short side, or stop and come back to deke the goalie on the short side. Make them skate past the net and back-hand the puck, so that the goalie learns to follow them. If they try to trick him in this exercise, his confidence may be badly shaken. Give him a chance to improve, and as he does, he will learn to protect himself against these moves.

Results

This exercise teaches the *forwards* to skate 'way past the goal to deke the goalie (which the better players do), to slow down before shooting the puck from their back-hand position, to lift the puck rather than slide it on the ice, and to go for the possible rebound, rather than skate away after they shoot.

Deking the goalie

The *goalie* practices:

following the puck carrier from a crouch position, moving with and toward the player, not backward into the net,

pushing with the back foot,

transferring his weight from one leg to the other,

playing his angles in case of a shot and adjusting if the player decides to cross in front of the net; he must stand up, not fall down, because the player will sometimes stop and come back to the short side;

poking the puck away from the player if he stops to come back on the short side,

controlling rebounds and clearing the puck away from the front of the net.

Do not hold this practice too long, and give your goalie a chance to regain his net before sending another player in. If you have two goalies, change every five rushes.

Don't practice this if your goalie is a bad skater; he will then dive at the puck, flop on the ice every time, and lose his confidence.

The goalie should always stand up. If he moves correctly with the puck carrier, he should be able to stop him most of the time.

Remember that hockey is a game of mistakes, and you will have to repeat your instructions as long as you coach. The more patient you are, the more success you'll have.

When a player, even a star, does not obey, bench him. if that doesn't work, trade him. If he stays, he will upset the morale of your team, and his mistakes will cost your team a lot of games.

9 HOW TO CHOOSE A GOALIE

It is most important that you give considerable thought to the choice of goalies and that you find out beforehand what they're made of.

Their playing records account for most of their points, but consider, too, the environment they live in, their marks at school, the friends they go out with, the hours they keep. These factors can adversely affect some players to the point where they fall short of what you are looking for.

Take time to consider what every candidate does on and off the ice, compare their records, and sign the ones with the best all-'round results. These ones are usually the "fighters" who have the will to win, the desire so necessary for success in the net.

Since goalies are vital members of your team, and good ones are at a premium, don't let one slip through your hands for lack of information. The more you know about them, the better you'll be able to help them, and consequently, the more they will contribute to the success of your team.

The guidelines that follow do not apply to beginners, because they have no records to be used as a reference. It is only a suggested checklist of points to consider before inviting a young man to your training camp. Some of the requirements can be amended or eliminated, depending on your situation and the age of the goalie.

Here, not necessarily in order of importance, are the questions to ask yourself about a prospective goalie.

1 **Is he a quitter?** Playing goal when a team is leading is easy, but when it falls behind, the pressure mounts to the point where some goalies can't stand it and stop trying. Without realizing why, they get mad at their teammates and tend to blame them for the goals instead of working harder.

Sometimes they'll just have a bad day and the goals will pour in, but other times, a key save lifts the team up and starts a rally. If goalies remember this, they can more easily overcome their letdown. But if after they learn that a slump is only temporary they do not change, they are lacking the desire needed to produce a star goalie, the one with the mark of champion.

2. **Does he practice hard?** Quitting during games is often the result of bad spirit during practices. One plays as be practices, and the goalie who sloughs off the daily workout will often turn in a lacklustre performance during the games and blame his teammates for his lack of success. Furthermore, if he doesn't try hard in practice, his teammates will have no challenge, and they'll have less enthusiasm.

3. **Is he liked by his teammates?** Since goalies represent between 50 to 65 per cent of their team, it is most important that they get along with their teammates. If there is constant friction between them, their cooperation and teamwork will be badly affected. Arguments can always happen, but they must be quickly forgotten. A grudge can ruin the best team.

4. **Is he punctual?** The goalie is a must for practices and games. When he is late, or doesn't show up, nothing goes. If he is often late, find out why. It may be that he just needs a lift to practice. However, if he is indifferent and just too lazy to show up on time, he means trouble. He doesn't care enough about the game to make the sacrifices necessary to win. He comes first, and the team second. In a team game, stay away from these players as much as possible.

5. **Can he take criticism?** Some players cannot accept advice without offering all sorts of excuses to cover their mistakes. Sometimes their reasons are valid, but constant objection to criticism is annoying. Coaches hate this kind of player and eventually give up on them, which is bad for the spirit of a team.

6. **Is he distracted by the fans?** Everything out of the ordinary adds pressure on a team, especially when a goalie reacts to a hostile crowd. People tease him to provoke him and make him play poorly. If he answers them, they'll try it again every time he plays there. If the goalie can't learn to ignore the crowd, they'll get on his nerves more and more and hurt his game to the point where it will reflect on the rest of the team.

7. **Can he follow the puck?** A lot of goalies play very well when they see the puck, but cannot follow it on screen shots. They either stand up behind the players or fall on the ice, hoping the puck will hit them. Then, they look up reproachfully at their teammates, as if to say, "I couldn't see the puck because of you." It's an excuse for not working hard enough; in today's hockey, if a goalie can't bend down to find the puck and follow it between the players' legs, he won't survive very long, and he doesn't belong in the net.

8. **Is he alert?** The better goalies are alert at all times—to follow the puck, to move with it, to notice player changes as the play goes on, and to leave their nets to play the puck. There is a difference between being alert and overly aggressive. When a goalie is too aggressive, he sometimes takes foolish chances and becomes careless. This eventually backfires on him.

9. **Does he talk to his team-mates?** The goalie should always talk to his players and direct the traffic. He should tell them when an opponent is open in front of the net or where to pass the puck. This will help his team control the puck better and can often mean the difference between a win and a loss.

10. **Is he an angle goalie?** Now that almost every player uses the slap shot, angle goalies should have more success than reflex goalies because they leave a smaller opening, have to move very little to make a save, can play the rebounds more easily, and can go after the loose pucks faster.

11. **Does he go back on the shots?** Some angle goalies tend to move back as the players come toward them, thus opening a bigger hole for them to shoot at. This tendency is sometimes the sign of a fear of slap shots. If not, it can be corrected quite easily with the proper coaching.

12. **Is he a good skater?** Skating ability is very important, because it affects balance, which in turn controls the way the goalie stops the puck and goes after it outside his net. A bad skater will not stand properly. Because he can't switch his weight from the balls of his feet to the front or back of his skates, he will offset his balance. He will fall down often, stay there too long, and give a lot of rebounds.

13. **Does he give rebounds?** Rebounds are costly when the goalie leaves them in front of the net. They are usually the result of the goalie's using the wrong stance and being off balance, making him push his pad forward with each shot and push his stick at the same time. Dropping one knee to the ice to make a save also sends the puck in front of the goal line; if the puck hits the stick on such a save, it will rebound almost directly back to the shooter, because the stick is resting on the skate and faces the puck instead of being turned on an angle to deflect the puck to the side.

14. **Does he have a good glove hand?** The catching glove is the goalie's bread and butter, and he must know how to use it to his advantage. Those who don't will never be too successful.

15. **Does he use his back-hand glove properly?** The back-hand glove is used as much as the catching glove, but coaches don't

notice it as much because the play doesn't stop after a backhand save. It is very important to master the use of the backhand glove, because that hand also controls the stick.

16. **How does he use his stick?** The stick is so useful that all goalies should learn everything there is to know about it for better results. The wrong stick can affect a goalie's stance, the way he controls rebounds, and the way he plays loose pucks. His effectiveness can sometimes be improved with a stick of, different proportions and lie.

17. **Can he follow an opponent across the goal mouth?** Following the puck carrier across the goal mouth is not easy, because the opponent can do so many things with the puck. Some goalies never learn to defend themselves against these plays, and because of that some other part of their game, such as the back-band, may be adversely affected. If the goalie is too apprehensive on these plays, he will anticipate the shot and flop to the ice before the shot is taken or stand straight up, leaving the bottom of the net open.

18. **Does he use the "V" or butterfly style?** This style is not easy to master. Those who don't use it properly tend to make the first move, stay on the ice too long, and give a lot of rebounds, and they can't clear the loose pucks away. To know more about it read the section covering that style.

These are some of the qualifications I would look for if I had to choose a goalie. But I would place a different emphasis on some points, depending on the age of the goalie. You can't judge the younger ones as you do the older ones; the latter should have most of the moves, while the smaller ones are still learning.

This list should help you to choose the best goalie available, the one you hope will carry your team to the championship. Don't forget to include all the factors—on and off the ice—for a more complete and accurate analysis.

APPENDIX
EQUIPMENT CHECKLIST

Playgrounds and arenas should provide a variety of sizes for every piece of equipment. The supervisor should check the equipment after each use, making sure it is properly dried. He should keep the following in mind with regard to purchase and care of equipment.

SKATES

Goalies' skates are expensive, but with proper care they last and last. If you rent or supply them it is most important that rivets and eyelets be checked each time the skates are returned.

PADS

It is critical that pads be the right size. Keep a good selection available. When they are returned, check the toe straps and look for possible holes in the leather to ensure that the padding does not come out.

CHEST PROTECTOR

Buy different sizes so that each goalie can be fitted properly.

The correct length is to the waist.

SHOULDER PADS

It is important that the padding be substantial both inside and outside of the arms. Still the goalies must be able to move freely—a tall goalie must not be given short pads and vice-versa.

CATCHING GLOVE

The pocket must be protected and the size must be just right. The glove should never be dried on a radiator, and should be oiled monthly.

BACK-HAND GLOVE

Holes in the palm of the back-hand glove must be repaired immediately. The hand part should be changed when the leather starts to irritate. Remember that the fingers must be free to grab the stick firmly; cut the finger loops from under the back piece.

STICKS

If you buy hockey sticks, buy one brand only for each lie and size so that the goalies have the same feeling every game.

MASKS

The mask must cover all of the head and have a back piece to replace the helmet in order to ensure maximum safety.